THE HOSPITAL IN THE OATFIELD

The Art of Nursing in the First World War

EDITED BY NATASHA McENROE & TIG THOMAS

EDITORIAL CONSULTANT: CHRISTINE E HALLETT

Florence **NIGHTINGALE MUSEUM**

Published by the Florence Nightingale Museum

2 Lambeth Palace Road, London SE1 7EW

First published in 2014

Foreword © Elizabeth Millicent, Countess of Sutherland 2014

The Redoubtable Millicent, Duchess of Sutherland and her Hospital under Canvas © Simon Chaplin and Natasha McEnroe 2014

Doctor Morgan text within Chapter 1 © Louise Skioldebrand 2014

Allan Hamilton text within Chapter 1 © Carr-Gomm 2014

'It is the Nurse who Does the Work' © Emily Mayhew 2014

An Insistent Duty © Sue Light 2014

'The Elite' © Eric Gruber von Arni 2014

Traumas of Conflict © Christine Hallett 2014

Ten Paintings of the Hospital in the Oatfield by Victor Tardieu (1915) © Danuta Kneebone 2014

The Stylish Nurse © Frederic A Sharf and Jill Carey 2014

All the Living and All the Dead © Holly Carter-Chappell 2014

Vera Brittain text on pages 22, 67, 92 © the estate of Vera Brittain 1970

Enid Bagnold text on pages 20, 26, 30, 36, 82 © the estate of Enid Bagnold

All other text © Natasha McEnroe 2014

Production by Strange Attractor Press (www.strangeattractor.co.uk)

Design and layout by Emerald Mosley (www.emeraldmosley.com)

Cover design Emerald Mosley (www.emeraldmosley.com)

Printed in England by CPI Antony Rowe

Contents

FOREWORD by Elizabeth Millicent, Countess of Sutherland ix

1. THE REDOUBTABLE MILLICENT, DUCHESS OF SUTHERLAND AND
HER HOSPITAL UNDER CANVAS
Simon Chaplin and Natasha McEnroe 1

2. 'IT IS THE NURSE WHO DOES THE WORK'
Field Hospitals in the First World War
Emily Mayhew 15

3. AN INSISTENT DUTY
Voluntary and Professional Nursing Services 1914-1919
Sue Light 25

4. 'THE ELITE'
Queen Alexandra's Imperial Military Nursing Service in the First World War
Eric Gruber von Arni 35

5. TRAUMAS OF CONFLICT
Nursing the Wounded of the First World War
Christine Hallett 63

6. TEN PAINTINGS OF THE HOSPITAL IN THE OATFIELD BY VICTOR
TARDIEU (1915)
Danuta Kneebone 71

7. THE STYLISH NURSE 1914-1918
Frederic A Sharf and Jill Carey 81

8. ALL THE LIVING AND ALL THE DEAD
How the First World War Changed our View of Death
Holly Carter-Chappell 89

Epilogue 99
Acknowledgements 100
Bibliography 101
Author Biographies 104

What I thought would be for me an impossible task became absolutely natural: to wash wounds, to drag off rags and clothing soaked in blood, to soothe a soldier's groans, to raise a wounded man while he was receiving extreme unction, hemmed in by nuns and a priest, so near he seemed to death; these actions seemed suddenly to become an insistent duty, perfectly easy to carry out. —**Millicent, Duchess of Sutherland**

To the nurses of the First World War
who fought so bravely to save lives

Foreword

•◆•

I was delighted to learn of the new interest in my grandmother Millicent Sutherland's nursing work in the Great War. She was more like a mother to me than a grandmother, as my own parents died young and she took their place. My grandmother sometimes shared with me her memories of her time in the hospital in the oatfield in France, and we would look through her photo albums together. Despite the horrors of war, she remembered it as a happy time in her life, when both professional and volunteer nurses worked together to care for the wounded men. Her own daughter and her daughter-in-law volunteered as nurses and worked alongside her, as did various other friends.

My grandmother always loved to help people. I remember an occasion when I was at school outside Vienna in the 1930s, and my grandmother came to stay for a few days to see me. She discovered that the man who sold the newspapers outside the hotel was Jewish, and he was terribly worried for his safety. Characteristically, my grandmother managed to arrange for him and his family to leave the country, and I still have his grateful letters of thanks to her. She was an extremely determined person. If she wanted to do something, she would just wait until you let her do it.

I think that my grandmother's wartime nursing work was partly inspired by her affection for France, where she lived after the war until her death. She spoke French well, and her grave at the family seat Dunrobin Castle in the Northern Highlands is marked with the Cross of Lorraine.

I am so glad that the oil paintings of my grandmother's hospital camp by Victor Tardieu are now at the Florence Nightingale Museum at St Thomas' Hospital. I have happy memories of St Thomas', as I myself worked as a laboratory technician there during the Second World War.

Elizabeth Millicent, Countess of Sutherland

1

The Redoubtable Millicent, Duchess of Sutherland and her Hospital under Canvas

·•·

Simon Chaplin and Natasha McEnroe

Sometimes it takes an artist, rather than a historian or biographer, to open a window on the past. A series of remarkable paintings by Victor Tardieu of the field hospital run by Millicent, Countess of Sutherland captures a moment of tranquillity and transformation amid the turmoil of the First World War, and provides one such time tunnel. The paintings give pause for thought about the contribution of the thousands of nurses who were drawn into the conflict. If the Crimea is famous for the work of Florence Nightingale and her subsequent efforts to professionalise nursing, then the First World War marks a further turning point, in which women nurses had once more to fight against prejudice and bureaucracy. This volume, and the exhibition which it accompanies, are a celebration and commemoration of their work, as exemplified by a woman who was described as a 'modern Nightingale' for her efforts to bring care to those who most needed it.

Given the experiences in the Crimea six decades earlier, and the subsequent advances made by women nurses, it may seem surprising that alongside the real battles a quieter fight against medical authority took place during the First World War. By the end of the 1880s nursing sisters were routinely employed in all British army hospitals with 100 or more beds. Some 1400 nurses served in South Africa during the Boer War, but with the return of peace the number soon dropped. Although the Queen Alexandra's Imperial Military Nursing Service, founded at the beginning of the twentieth century, provided a formal structure for female nurses, active military medical care was primarily a male domain, with women mostly designated as reservists to be called up only in time of conflict, alongside the male reservists of the Royal Army Medical Corps.

The call came, of course, in August 1914. The outbreak of hostilities prompted a huge increase in women volunteers, trained and untrained. Many of the latter joined the Voluntary Aid Detachment (VAD) to become nurses, and these women—often from relatively protected backgrounds—worked closely with professional nurses who acted as teachers and mentors to the VADs. It was a highly stressful and often dangerous environment. Even experienced peacetime army nurses were unprepared for the scale of the task facing them, and to the threat of disease or injury was added the ever-present risk of physical and nervous exhaustion. Yet the war, and nursing in particular, also offered unprecedented opportunities for women, and middle- and upper-class women in particular seized the opportunity to assume a degree of independence previously denied them. Not surprisingly, many chafed against the rigid and sometimes short-sighted approach of the regular army medical service and some demonstrated considerable initiative, bravery and occasionally guile to circumvent authority when required, in ways that would have been unthinkable to regular army personnel.

One such woman was Millicent Fanny St Clair-Erskine (1867-1955), the first daughter of the 4th Earl of Rosslyn. A precocious society beauty, Millicent was married to the Duke of Sutherland on her seventeenth birthday, and she somewhat mutinously bore their first child nine months later. Three further children soon followed, and, her reproductive duties done, Sutherland devoted all her time to entertaining and fundraising for worthy causes. As a hostess, she is described admiringly by Vita Sackville-West in *The Edwardians* (1930): 'Millie looking like a goddess, with a golden train halfway down the stairs. The charm of that woman!' Whilst greeting guests, Sutherland would hold a sheaf of lilies as a way of avoiding shaking hundreds of hands—a striking contrast to the enforced intimacy of her later role as a military nurse. She was not, however, simply a socialite butterfly. Instead she was possessed of a strong social conscience, which she applied in a series of campaigns aimed at achieving better working conditions in the Potteries, near her husband's seat at Trentham in Staffordshire. Her interest in reform sat uneasily with some who saw her as an embarrassment to both her class and her gender, earning her the nickname 'Meddlesome Millie'. She was also caricatured in the novels of Arnold Bennett as 'Irritating Iris', the 'Countess of Chell', whose behaviour so frequently exasperated the conservative councillors of the Five Towns. In reality, her charitable work was highly practical: training local women as midwives, setting up The Cripples Guild of Handicrafts and campaigning against the use of lead in the Potteries.

'Sister Millicent'—The Duchess in her working uniform, France 1914. Her chatelaine for scissors and other nursing equipment is at her waist. Photographer: Oswald Gayer Morgan. Reproduced by courtesy of Louise and Robert Skioldebrand.

Widowhood in 1913 gave the Duchess increased independence. Five days after war was declared, she departed to France to establish an ambulance unit, the first of several such units to be set up by upper- and middle-class British women. The Sutherland Field Ambulance was an individual response to a pressing medical need resulting from the inadequacy of professional military medical services, and Millicent Sutherland's earlier campaigning on social issues translated into a personal mission that often brought her into conflict with the army medical establishment. Under the auspices of the French Red Cross, Sutherland, together with the surgeon Oswald Gayer Morgan and eight British nurses, travelled from Paris to Namur in Belgium in the late summer of 1914. There they set up a small hospital in the convent of *Les Soeurs de Notre Dame* to nurse French and Belgian troops. As Namur fell to the German forces, the nurses and nuns worked to care for the victims of the terrible shelling. 'No one, until these awful things happen,' wrote the Duchess, 'can conceive of the untold value of a fully trained and disciplined British nurse.' Trapped under German occupation, she managed to talk her way out through a combination of her forceful personality and

I had just buried my revolver under an apple tree when the bombardment began once more. The church bells were ringing for vespers. Then whizz! bang! come the shells over our heads again. Picric acid and splinters fall at our very feet. We can see German soldiers running for dear life. Can it be the French artillery that is driving them out? — Millicent, **Duchess of Sutherland**

judicious reference to her pre-war friendship with the German Crown Prince. By taking a circuitous route back to Britain via Holland, she and her nurses escaped occupied territory in a dramatic journey.

On her return, Sutherland remained in England only long enough to marry Percy Fitzgerald, her lover of the previous ten years,

and to write an autobiographical account of her experiences in order to raise funds to continue her mission. Her book, *Six Weeks at the War*, was published by *The Times* and, like the same paper's accounts of the work of Nightingale, it

The Sutherland Ambulance Unit on their escape from occupied Belgian, September 1914. Millicent Sutherland, Oswald Gayer Morgan, eight nurses and the manager of their hotel at The Hague. The Duchess's flowers are tied with Dutch and Belgium national colours. Reproduced by courtesy of Louise and Robert Skioldebrand.

captured the public imagination. With her coffers replenished and her energy restored, Sutherland returned to the continent in October 1914, with a larger contingent of nurses, surgeons and drivers. After initially setting up a hospital of 100 beds at Malo-les-Bains near Dunkirk, the French authorities made the decision to transfer her hospital inland to temporary accommodation at Bourbourg in the spring of 1915 as the shelling along the coastline increased.

The camp in the oatfield, as it was known to the locals, demonstrated the ingenuity of the nursing and medical staff. Sutherland had already ordered tents and canvas, but the shelter was extended by brightly coloured awnings borrowed from the many hotels along the Malo seafront.

Panorama of Bourbourg camp, 1915. The larger marquees and smaller tents lie in the protection of the slight valley of the oatfield. Photographer: Oswald Gayer Morgan. Reproduced by courtesy of Louise and Robert Skioldebrand.

An anonymous nurse described the hospital in *The Field* magazine, giving a useful record of some of the practical details:

> The hospital is run on very business-like methods, but has, at the same time, a home-like and picturesque appearance. The tents are painted … artistically to defy detection from the air, and they are planted round with simple bright flowers. There is an operation, and an X-ray tent. The staff is perpetually occupied, for when it is a matter of dealing with private and not public money there is no question of overstaffing. The hospital consists of a matron, fourteen fully trained and paid nurses, four experienced Voluntary Aid Detachments, and two probationers; there is also a lady secretary, a chaplain and two

or three gentlemen who render valuable assistance in driving cars. The two surgeons, who were trained at Guy's Hospital and Edinburgh Infirmary, are assisted by one dresser from the Middlesex Hospital. There are Belgian and British orderlies, but the latter are chiefly lads under military age trained at the Technical School in Sutherland. There is a kitchen staff of women. A French doctor is attached who keeps all permissions and papers relating to the patients and arranges for their transference to hospitals further from the fighting line, for this camp is only a few miles from the British lines and within earshot of the guns on the Belgian frontier [the second Battle of Ypres was taking place just 40 miles to the east]. Millicent, Duchess of Sutherland has made no public appeal for funds as she considers that a voluntary hospital, although attached to the French Army Medical Service, should not divert support from British hospitals run by national organisations; on the other hand, this ambulance has done such continuous and useful work, that she has been supported privately in a very remarkable degree, and has also received many gifts in kind, such as medical dressings, warm clothing, linen, eggs, flour, butter...

Although it was in existence for only a few months before Sutherland moved to a new and larger site, the appearance of the camp in all its colourful glory was captured for posterity by the French artist Victor Tardieu (1870-1937). Tardieu is now best known for his role as founder and first director of the École des Beaux-Arts de l'Indochine in Hanoi in the late 1920s and early 1930s, and for his part in the emergence of a distinctive school of artists who blended the technical skills of European Impressionism with South-East Asian techniques and aesthetic influences (see Chapter 6). Tardieu was attached to the American Field Service (AFS), a volunteer ambulance driver unit. Although he initially had no official role as an artist Tardieu continued to paint, taking every opportunity his duties and the weather offered. His work with the AFS brought him into contact with Sutherland and her hospital and, encouraged by the Duchess, he made a number of paintings of the hospital and its patients and nurses.

These small oil paintings, which are now held by the Florence Nightingale Museum, are finely executed and highly accomplished works. As open-air scenes they demonstrate a mastery of the use of oils to create colour and texture, not least in the handling of late summer light to capture the translucency of fabric, foliage and skin, conveying a sense of delicacy and fragility that is echoed by the bodies of the recuperating soldiers. Just as some of Tardieu's pre-war dockyard paintings used dark colours, strong shadows and lines to emphasise the physical labour of working men, here the lightness

A WINDY NIGHT—BUT THE PRECIOUS THERMOMETERS ARE SAVED

One of the many challenges of life in a field hospital was the occasional collapse of tents, which unsettled patients and caused breakages of vital medical equipment. Illustration by R M Savage 'and others', Olive Dent's *A VAD in France*, 1917

of touch—not least in the depiction of Sutherland herself, in white nurse's dress and coif—serves the opposite purpose, emphasising the gentleness of the carers and the incapacity of their patients. Whether by accident or intent the depiction of bruised skies, thundery light, ripe oats ready for harvest and the profusion of flowers growing wild, in tubs or in vases by the bedside also creates a slightly ominous feeling of change. This sense of foreboding is also manifest in the pensive attitudes of those soldiers whose recuperation is more advanced, and who—in their dark uniform jackets—appear to be already thinking of what might yet lie in store for them.

More prosaically, the paintings also document Sutherland's adherence to a model of nursing which sought to redress, or at least contain, psychological, as well as physical, trauma by creating environments conducive to healing. Evident in nursing practice before the war, but brought to greater prominence after 1914, the approach is described in manuals such as Violetta Thurstan's *A*

Text Book of War Nursing, published in 1917. Thurstan stressed the importance of fresh air and ventilation for healing to take place. Although Sutherland was no more prominent in this regard than any of her contemporaries, nonetheless the attention to the surroundings in which her patients recuperated is strikingly apparent in Tardieu's work.

Tetanus appeared, but we soon obtained serums from England and gave all patients with wounds covering large surfaces a preventative injection. Often large pieces of clothing were embedded in wounds, to say nothing of shrapnel and mud. From beneath one man's shoulder blade we even extracted a large brass time-fuse!
—Anon, author of *A War Nurse's Diary*

An anonymous nurse who briefly stayed with the Sutherland Ambulance Unit later wrote: 'The surgeon said the only way to be sure of the mischief not spreading was to cut off his leg. I begged him to allow me to syringe it every half hour and meanwhile I removed him outside in the winter sunshine, fixing his leg up so that the air played all around the wound and left it absolutely exposed all day long. It did well, and the gangrene came off in one big slough, leaving fresh, red flesh underneath.' The extremes of war caused a temporary blurring of roles for women, who under the pressure of active conflict frequently crossed the lines between surgery and nursing. It also offered nurses the opportunities to develop expertise never before available to them. A nurse who carried out the duty of cleaning wounds would remove pieces of shrapnel and shell, and daily examinations would also involve picking out pieces of dirt or clothing as they rose to the surface. In an emergency, an experienced nurse would even carry out a minor surgical operation. From the second half of the war, nurses were trained as anaesthetists, only to have this role removed from them after the Armistice.

Crucial to the work of the Sutherland Field Hospital were the surgeons Oswald Gayer Morgan (1889-1981) and Major Allan George Hamilton (1885-1972). Hamilton served as House Surgeon at the Edinburgh Royal Infirmary, before moving to the Hospital for Women in Liverpool, and Morgan worked at Guy's Hospital, to which he returned after the war, having gained considerable practical experience from his work in France. He was an early adopter of the Carrel-Dakin method of wound irrigation, an important treatment in the days before penicillin. The Carrel-Dakin method helped prevent the spread of infections such as gas-gangrene, common in soldiers wounded on the Western Front, by using sodium hypochlorite to clean wounds.

The method involved the fluid being stored in a glass jar at the head of the bed, and then carried away down a rubber tube, into a smaller glass tube with several rubber nozzles that were placed into the wound in different places and bandaged over to keep them in place. Tubes were changed every two days, and swabs were tested for any infection before the wound was closed. To be a success, the method needed constant monitoring and recording from the nurse. Sutherland and her nurses received training in this method at Carrel-Dakin Hospital in Compiègne. 'There was a fascination in watching the way

Ward with patients undergoing the Carrel-Dakin method of wound irrigation, Calais, 1917. Photographer: Oswald Gayer Morgan. Reproduced by courtesy of Louise and Robert Skioldebrand.

the wound grew less dirty-yellow and more bright-red beneath the cleansing stream,' wrote Irene Rathbone, a young actress who served as a VAD. This and other ground-breaking treatments such as portable storage of blood for transfusions and mobile X-ray equipment played a major role in improving the chances of survival for those injured in the latter half of the war.

As well as being a pioneering surgeon, Morgan was also a talented amateur photographer, who took his camera with him to the hospital in the oatfield. His collection of photographs provides a fascinating and informal record of daily life of the nurses, doctors and patients, delightfully demonstrating the enforced intimacy of camp life. In addition to the professional nurses and doctors, some of Millicent Sutherland's own family and friends volunteered to serve in the Sutherland unit, adding to the informal atmosphere. One volunteer nurse was Sutherland's own daughter, Lady Rosemary, who nursed for several years during the war.

Nurses in field hospitals were close enough to the fighting to get a real sense of the experience of the soldiers in the trenches, and the camp so beautifully depicted in the Tardieu paintings and Morgan photographs would have been near enough to Dunkirk to hear the shelling. The trauma experienced by the soldiers in the First World War is well documented, but its impact on nurses was no less profound. In *A Diary without Dates* (1918) Enid Bagnold describes a sister as 'white and shaking' as she was taken off duty due to shock. In addition to treating combat injuries and the ever-present risk of gas gangrene, nurses on the Western Front were also confronted with patients suffering the terrible and distressing effects of poison gas.

In this respect, perhaps, the serenity of the hospital in the oatfield depicted by Tardieu belies the gruelling physical and emotional demands of wartime nursing. Nevertheless, as works of art and as documentary sources they provide an unparalleled insight into a war that will soon pass beyond living memory. The hospital, and the paintings that form such a remarkable record

After Bourbourg, the Sutherland Unit transferred to Calais, where in 1917 it received a royal visit. Lady Rosemary, daughter of Millicent Sutherland, stands to the left of the Prince of Wales. © Imperial War Museums Q2585.

of it, mark the turning of a season as well as a significant period of military nursing. The camp was only three months in existence: at summer's end, the hospital was moved to a series of huts in the dunes of Calais and became part of the British Red Cross. Millicent Sutherland nursed in France until the end of the war, and Tardieu left with the American Ambulance Field Service, during which time he was commissioned to produce war posters used to generate funds from the American public. The paintings from Bourbourg, however, remained treasured personal possessions of Sutherland, a gift to 'Madame la Duchesse' from 'un simple soldat'. A century on, it is fitting that some of these wonderful works should have found a home in the Florence Nightingale Museum, which is devoted not just to the memory of one wartime nurse, but to the history of nursing in peace and conflict over almost two centuries.

Jean Carr-Gomm, Allan Hamilton's daughter writes: my father, Allan Hamilton MD FRCS Edin, was born in New Zealand, one of fourteen children. He always wanted to be a doctor and his wish came true when in 1904 he qualified as a surgeon. In October 1914 he joined the Millicent Sutherland Ambulance Unit as a volunteer surgeon and was responsible for actually taking out the X-ray equipment when the unit went to France. There he worked as a surgeon, together with Dr Morgan, at the camp in the oatfield, which was run by Millicent, Duchess of Sutherland. When the camp in the oatfield was disbanded in October 1915 he joined the Royal Army Medical Corps. After the war ended he set up practice as a GP in a house opposite the Brompton Hospital, as he was unable to be a surgeon in London with an Edinburgh degree. Starting with only one patient, he built up what was to become the largest general practice in London. He also worked voluntarily three afternoons a week at the Royal College of St Katherine—an early welfare centre. At that time, rickets was rife, and my father spent much of his time amongst the East End mothers, attempting to educate them about preventative diet. This eventually led him to make a film about the causes of rickets and its prevention, with the aim of reaching a wider audience. He continued to practise until 1946 and died peacefully aged 87.

Louise Skioldebrand, Morgan's granddaughter, writes: Grandpa was a charming, moderate, modest and generous gentleman. The more we discover about him, the more I realise his amazing strengths. An obviously well-educated man (Epsom College, Clare College Cambridge and Guy's Hospital), he was passionate about his gardens and collected some beautiful pieces of art and furniture over the years.

He won awards for his gardens both in London and Walberswick, Suffolk. I found his war medals amongst his medical lecture medals and also one for his London garden in St John's Wood. When he went on various travels he would often manage to bring back a little cutting of some rare plant (probably illegally, but he could usually twinkle his way out of any trouble!), which he would then nurture and enjoy in his garden.

He had a beautiful singing voice and appreciated classical music with a passion. This artistic streak came out in his daughter, Janet, and he acquired some beautiful pieces of art including a Tardieu oil and a charcoal drawing of a Tunisian soldier at the Sutherland Unit. I have the privilege of enjoying a large Flemish oak dresser in our dining room, which he acquired from a grateful patient during the First World War. The story is that he helped a local farmer, who said he must have something from his house as a token of his appreciation. Grandpa chose this sizeable piece of furniture and got it shipped over to England during the war. The original sixteen panes of glass remain intact to this day!

I now realise that his photos are rather well done … perhaps his understanding of the camera lens helped him to become the acclaimed ophthalmologist he was.

I see that his experiences during the First World War must have given him great leadership skills … even if that might not have been by choice. He went on to be president of the Ophthalmological Society in 1954 and a vice-president of the British Medical Association in 1965 and was an acclaimed lecturer, not afraid of being anti-establishment when he could see an innovative way of working.

He was a devoted and supportive father to his two daughters, Sheena (our mother) and Janet, having the tragic experience of losing their mother to an incurable illness in 1938. He never married again, but threw his energy into his work and into debating, and writing, not only on his academic work but also, in retirement, about penal reform, euthanasia and spiritual life. Throughout his life he enjoyed his gardens, music, wine and family.

2

"It is the Nurse who Does the Work"
Field Hospitals in the First World War

•◆•

Emily Mayhew

Tardieu's paintings of the Sutherland Ambulance facility are testimony not just to the work of the extraordinary men and women who served there but also to an entirely new type of military medical provision. The 'camp in the oatfield', portrayed so vividly and with such detailed care, was one of many hospitals in many fields that were improvised hurriedly in late 1914 and early 1915 in response to the crisis of casualty on the Western Front. Improvisation did not mean sub-standard casualty care. These field hospitals, along with the Casualty Clearing Stations and base hospitals of the official medical services, were the forerunners of many of the military medical units of the modern times. Tardieu's work provides us with some of the earliest images of this cornerstone of casualty care; its importance as both artistic and medical record is therefore significant.

By October 1914, when Millicent Sutherland was heading back out to France with her staff of surgeons and nurses, the entire military medical system was in chaos. It was not poor planning. The British military medical authorities had extensive experience in providing for sick and wounded soldiers from their colonial wars. They had surgeons and doctors who had served in the Boer Wars in South Africa, and who were keen to put that experience to good use in France. A network of base hospitals had been built along the French coast ready to receive casualties. They were large and fully equipped along the lines of the most modern civilian facilities back in Britain. The problem was that war itself had changed beyond recognition or anticipation.

From the outset, the weapons used in France and Belgium created wounds that were unprecedentedly severe. Gone were the neat holes caused by rounded ammunition that flew slowly, could be easily located and extracted, and did not leave much damage behind. Instead the new cylindro-conical bullets, fired by powerful new guns, hit fast and hard, went deep and took bits of dirty uniform and airborne soil particles in with them. Inside the human body, bullets ricocheted off bones and ploughed through soft tissue until their energy was spent. Shrapnel fragments, eventually the cause of most of the war's injuries, were every bit as bad. They created jagged wounds that bled profusely and, if the casualty survived long enough, provided the perfect environment for sepsis and infection. In South Africa most of the men in the military wards had been suffering from disease, with severely wounded casualties being the exception for the doctors who treated them. In France, the exception became

Model of First World War field hospital camp bed. Reproduced by courtesy of Wellcome Library, London.

the norm. Oswald Morgan, the surgeon who accompanied Millicent Sutherland to France and worked in the hospital, was one of those who realised they would be working in a completely new casualty environment. He hurriedly wrote an article for a medical journal in September 1914 to warn his colleagues who might follow him to France that 'the most serious wounds were caused by pieces of shell-casing, including the bone injuries, which were all comminuted factures, and so septic that in every case an incision was found necessary to remove loose pieces of bone, shell, and in some cases, clothing'.

It wasn't just the wounds that confounded surgeons like Morgan. The entire military medical system that had been implemented at the beginning of the war was incapable of providing an adequate response. The well-equipped base hospitals lay at the end of long roads, sixty miles or more away from the battlefield. Ambulance journeys took many hours and all too often when a driver arrived at a hospital everyone in the back of his vehicle had bled to death or died of shock on the way. Those that survived were frequently not strong enough for surgery; infections had already taken hold that could kill within days. Quickly it was realised that delay meant death, and speed was vital. Most of the wounds required surgery as close to the time of wounding as possible to stop the bleeding, extract the fragments of weapons and remove infected tissue. If the casualties could not get to the operating theatres in the base hospitals, then the hospitals would go to them.

So from January 1915 all along the Western Front surgeons took their teams and moved forward. It was a welcome surprise to many of them that they would not have to start entirely from scratch. There were medical facilities already in forward positions—the Casualty Clearing Stations—that were intended as a stopping point on the long evacuation journeys. They were usually constructed of long rows of tents, staffed by nurses and orderlies, and equipped to give out drinks and dressing changes. Casualty Clearing Station staff had found themselves at the sharp end of the war, inundated with casualties too weak to move on but with no supplies beyond cocoa and bandages to give them. They had seen off hundreds of casualties knowing

A " LINE " OF WARDS

This illustration shows the wooden walkways often used in field hospitals against the mud. Medical teams often put flowers and shrubs to brighten their environment. Illustration by R M Savage 'and others', Olive Dent's *A VAD in France*, 1917.

they would not survive the journey but that there was nothing else they could do. When the surgical teams arrived with their equipment, Casualty Clearing Station staff hurried to make space for them, creating operating theatres and pre- and post-op wards, and offering the kind of specialist care they had been desperate to provide.

Alongside the converted Casualty Clearing Stations were the new field hospitals, including the one created by Millicent Sutherland. Together an extraordinary new expert medical network was created all along the front, within earshot of the ever-pounding guns. Operating theatres were installed wherever they could fit—in hop houses, colleges, convents and in tents in oatfields. The results were immediate. Men who would otherwise have died lived. Surgeons in tents got results that would not have shamed a top London teaching hospital. And each of them knew that without their nurses, and their shared dedication to an entirely new way of treating battle casualties, none of it would have been possible. On the first day of the No1 Belgian Field Hospital opening in a forward position, surgeon Henry Souttar had ten ambulances full of badly wounded men, two scalpels, six artery forceps, two dissecting forceps and a finger saw. He also had a full team of nurses and, by nightfall,

Nurses outside a field hospital. The necessary camouflage against air attack can be clearly seen on the bell tents. © Imperial War Museums Q51883.

Nurse washing her hair in a basin outside her tent. Bourbourg camp, 1915. Photographer: Oswald Gayer Morgan. Reproduced by courtesy of Louise and Robert Skioldebrand.

everyone who could have been had been treated and saved. He knew who was responsible, saying: 'A physician gives his blessing, the surgeon does the operation. But it is the nurse who does the work.'

The nurses who had sought service in France were ready for the challenge of this work. They had arrived there from a range of different recruitment processes. There were the professional army nurses of the Queen Alexandra's Imperial Military Nursing Service. There were also professional nurses from civilian hospitals who had volunteered for military service through organisations such as the Red Cross, the Civil Hospital Reserve (also known as the Queen Alexandra's Imperial Military Nursing Service Reserve) and the Territorial Force Nursing Staff. They were fully trained and many held senior positions at their home hospitals. The greater their expertise, the more had been their frustration at not being able to help the soldiers in their care. These nurses provided the infrastructure on which the new field hospitals could be based. But there were not enough of them to sustain the new system going forward into the second year of the war. Volunteers from outside official nursing structures would be needed. The Voluntary Aid Detachment was the largest of these. They recruited volunteers for both nursing and orderly positions in the war. The volunteers then received medical training in a series of courses from the Red Cross and the St John Ambulance Association. Once in France, they came under the management of the professional nurses who aimed to supplement their training on the job. When the first ambulances rolled up to their tents, however, both groups of women knew they all had much more to learn, so together they rededicated themselves to the challenge.

Watchmakers, jewellers, station-masters, dress-designers, actors, travellers in underwear, bank clerks ... they come here in uniforms and we put them into pyjamas and nurse them; and they lie in bed or hobble about the ward, watching us as we move, accepting each other with the unquestioning faith of children. —Enid Bagnold, VAD nurse, author of *A Diary Without Dates*

However they got to the war, the nurses found they had one thing in common: they had not volunteered for military medical service to end up mopping floors and deferring to Sister. Instead, they aimed to demonstrate independence and initiative. Some discreetly wore the green and purple badge of the Suffragette movement pinned under their aprons, and had put aside the political aspects of the campaign to use nursing to demonstrate their fitness for full citizenship. Sutherland's biographies reveal that she too was intolerant of inflexible authorities' structures and traditions. The war would give them all a chance to become experts in their field—even if it was just an oatfield—trusted by their colleagues and crucial to the process by which hundreds of thousands of lives would be saved.

Henry Souttar was just one surgeon among many who understood that without the nurses none of the new military medical systems would work. From the moment a wounded man was admitted into a ward at a field hospital or Casualty Clearing Station, he depended for his life on his nurse. She worked with orderlies and bearers to remove the blood-soaked uniform, often little more than rags, and wash the battered soldier. For those in shock (the majority) and suffering from cold, blood loss, malnutrition and dehydration, it was the nurse who brought them back from the brink. Existing resuscitation techniques were refined and reworked to match the severity of the wounds of the casualties lying on the ward mattresses. Nurses learned to judge how much warm saline was needed subcutaneously, and to supplement it with sips of brandy and hot coffee, and quarter-grain doses of morphine. Hot-water bottles were placed all around a casualty grown cold from blood loss or exposure. Gradually men turned from shivering grey to calmer pink, their breathing steadied and they grew strong enough to raise their heads to receive further nourishment. From the resus ward, they could go to surgery with a fighting chance of coming out of theatre alive.

Resus was only the beginning. The new wounds of war were filthy, complex traumas needing constant care to prevent infection and sepsis spreading. This was the job of the nurse. Before surgery, nurses mixed up light chemical solutions and syringed them over the open wound sites to clean them and make the extent of the trauma visible for the surgeon. Surgery would remove the infected tissue and repair torn arteries and broken bones, and then the post-surgical wound would need to be kept clean and clear as it began the process of repair. The severity of wounds meant that cleaning often had to be done very frequently, sometimes on a half-hourly basis, each time involving dressing changes and pain for their soldier-casualty. It required detailed technical skill from the nurse who would also need to be speaking softly to her patient while working to keep him calm, and assure him of his recovery. It wasn't just the nurses of the Sutherland Ambulance who found their tented, rural location helpful in this process. Patients could be left in the fresh air and sunshine with their wounds open to help them heal. The open air, whilst cold in winter, also meant the wards were always well ventilated, the wind blowing away the smell of infections. Despite the demands of the work, most nurses flourished in this environment (although see Chapter 5 for details of the traumas they experienced). It was what they had always wanted from their job. There were no windows to wash or floors to mop. There were just men and their wounds and a very great sense of duty.

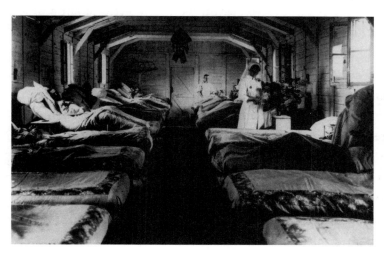

A Casualty Clearing Station. Nursing patients in very low camp beds was backbreaking work. Reproduced by courtesy of the Army Medical Services Museum.

Some patients required a nurse's attention for all their waking, suffering hours. Men who had received facial wounds, where their jaws or cheekbones had been damaged, were the greatest challenge of all. Surgeons needed to conserve as much of their wounded flesh as possible to be able to graft on replacement tissues so they could not cut away infected areas. Nurses therefore had to manage these wounds entirely on their own, by continual cleansing and redressing to keep infection at bay. To make their work even more complicated, these patients were usually unable to feed themselves, or indeed eat at all in a conventional manner. If they grew malnourished, surgeons would be unable to perform the complex reconstructive procedures that were required for face and jaw injuries. Nurses had to insert tubes into what was left of the patient's mouth and nose and then funnel in liquid nutrition—often concoctions of raw eggs, brandy and bouillon—past the wound site and directly down their throat. It was painful and inefficient; patients often coughed or retched during the process, splashing food all over their wounds. Nurses would stop, clean them carefully and begin again. A single meal could take hours. Patients grew deeply upset at the pain and indignity of their plight and the nurses had to keep their spirits up throughout, to convince them that it was all worth it and that if they persevered, the surgeon would be able to do his work. A surgeon's instruction to 'make him strong enough for surgery' in reality meant weeks of dedicated work on the part of the nurse. While we know of the pioneering reconstructive works of surgeons such as Harold Gillies, Charles Valadier and Hubert Morestin, we know little of the nurses who enabled them to operate in the first place, who steadied their patients in body and spirit and without whom no innovation would have been possible.

As for the wounds, I was growing accustomed to them; most of us, at that stage, possessed a kind of psychological shutter which we firmly closed down upon our recollection of the daily agony whenever there was time to think. —Vera Brittain, VAD nurse, author of *Testament of Youth*

It was not just the technical demands of nursing the severely wounded that nurses faced in field hospitals. There was just as much to learn and do outside the wards as there was in them. Field hospitals were unique environments, requiring both great expertise and a willingness to improvise in order to function. Nurses provided both. They learned how important it was to know what weather was coming. Tardieu painted the Sutherland Ambulance hospital on sunny days, when the canvas

Take down of Bourbourg camp in autumn 1915. The wooden bases that acted as flooring kept the tent interiors dry and also acted as insulation. Photographer: Oswald Gayer Morgan. Reproduced by courtesy of Louise and Robert Skioldebrand.

walls could be taken down, and light and air surround the patients. It wasn't always sunny: nurses learned to peg down tents so they wouldn't blow down on windy days and to tie doors firmly in place with ropes to keep out the rain. Despite the challenges of the environment, tented hospitals became the norm throughout the war—Tardieu's paintings therefore represent something typical, not anomalous. Tenting was flexible and easily modified. New wards could be put up in a couple of hours to meet the particular medical needs: for an outbreak of flu, of enteric disease or to provide wards for the dying in times of heavy casualties. Photographs of No 44 Field Hospital in Puchevillers, created before the offensives in the Somme of 1916, look very like the hospital in the oatfield, albeit less colourful. All its many wards were tented, with wooden floor sections keeping camp beds off the often damp and muddy ground. The Sutherland Ambulance hospital may only have existed for three months in the form Tardieu painted it, but it was part of an entire system that would last throughout the war.

From Tardieu's paintings we can also see other aspects of nursing care for patients and their environment, which would become part of daily medical

One welcomes any little need of the patient's. One poor boy one night whispered, 'I don't know what I want. I seem to be slipping away,' and at his request there were changed and changed again the pillows, the cushions, the position of the limb, the cradle, the bedclothes, his lips were moistened, his face wiped and then he spoke again. 'I know now why you nurses are called "sisters". You are sisters to us boys.' With a lump in the throat, and stinging tears at the back of the eyes one could only silently hope to ever be worthy of that name.
—Olive Dent, VAD nurse, author of *A VAD in France*

life along the Western Front. It was usually nurses who scrounged the few pieces of furniture to be found in their tented wards. Tardieu shows us the bedside tables and small folding stools where soldiers could keep their few possessions. Nurses found vases (often empty shell casings) and picked the flowers that grew in their rural surroundings. Tardieu shows bunches of red flowers—probably poppies—but in winter it was as likely to be holly or mistletoe. As war went on, nurses created long networks that stretched all the way back to Britain to ask for other items to bring their wind-buffeted wards to life. They had gramophones, magazines and books, and even bookcases sent from home. They sat by men whose lives they had saved with their resus mixtures and wrote letters home for them. They pressed the flowers they had put in vases and gave them for men to send to their sweethearts—for obvious reasons, forget-me-nots were always sought after. Sometimes they sat on the little folding stools by men who were waking after an operation to gently bring them to the knowledge that they had lost a limb, or two, and that their lives would never be the same again.

One ward in particular came to stand for all the new expertise learned and practised by the nurses of the First World War. The moribund ward was where soldiers who could not be saved went to die. No surgeons or doctors worked there, only nurses. It was nurses who saw the dying gently to their rest with as much comfort and dignity as could be found. They administered morphine to dull the pain. They sat for hours holding the hand of a soldier slipping away. They remembered his last words and wrote them down in 'break-the-news' letters for the families. They changed sheets and cleaned bloodstains. It was a dreadful place but nurses never shirked the responsibilities that they found there. Like all the other wards in the field hospitals of the Western Front, it was a place of great skill and dedication learned on site, in earshot of the guns, in oatfields and wheatfields, leaving a sturdy and extraordinary legacy for us today.

3

An Insistent Duty
Voluntary and Professional Nursing Services 1914–1919

•◆•

Sue Light

The women who served as nurses in the First World War belonged to several different organisations. The following is a brief description of the nursing services that worked under the auspices of the War Office, caring for members of the British Expeditionary Force and other nationalities in British military hospitals at home and abroad.

Queen Alexandra's Imperial Military Nursing Service (QAIMNS)
QAIMNS or the 'Regular' military nursing service was formed in 1902, soon after the general reorganisation of the Army Medical Services, and included many existing members of its forerunner, the Army Nursing Service

Standards for admission to the service were high, with women required to be between 25 and 35 years of age, British subjects, well-educated and having completed a three-year nurse training in an approved hospital. Most importantly, they had to persuade the Nursing Board that they were ladies of good social standing. In the main, they were the daughters of army officers, clergy, professional men, merchants and farmers. Interviews to weed out unsuitable candidates were rigorous. Some 1903-4 selection notes show reasons for rejection: Miss W P was merely 'too delicate for the work; could not go abroad', while Miss L D had 'an apparent want of social standing, and appearance unsuitable'. Miss W was rejected on the grounds that she was 'a coloured lady from America'; Miss N H was 'flippant' and Miss M M was 'quite unsuitable; father an iron-plate worker; mother cannot sign her name'.

Their working uniform consisted of grey dresses of 'washing' material for normal ward wear, with a scarlet cape, white cuffs and a white muslin cap, with the traditional floating 'wings' on either side of the head. Badges denoted rank and length of service, as did bands worn on the sleeve. Other than hemlines slowly rising, the ward uniform remained virtually unchanged until the Second World War.

A section of VADs and Military Nurses at No 2 Western General Hospital, Manchester during the First World War. Reproduced by courtesy of Sue Light.

Eight o'clock, nine o'clock … If only one could eat something! I took a sponge-finger out of a tin, resolving to pay it back out of my tea next day, and stole round to the dark corner near the German ward to eat it. The Germans were in bed; I could see two of them. At last, freed from their uniform, the dark blue with the scarlet soup-plates, they looked—how strange!—like other men. —Enid Bagnold, VAD nurse, author of *A Diary Without Dates*

During the First World War the relatively small number of permanent nurses in the QAIMNS remained unchanged, as it was considered unwise to employ more women permanently than would be needed after the end of the war. Any women who left the service were replaced, but the many thousands of nurses recruited during the war joined on short-term contracts with clauses that enabled the War Office to end their employment at its convenience.

Life in army hospitals during peacetime was very different from that in civil establishments. Military hospitals were, in general, small, with the majority having fewer than 200 beds, and the patients being mainly fit men under the age of 60, suffering from minor illness or the result of accidents.

No female probationers were employed, with male nursing orderlies of the Royal Army Medical Corps carrying out most of the care in the wards. The rather specialised and insular nature of the life produced a nursing service of educated and adventurous women, used to the ways of the army, but with little experience in the organisation and management of large, busy hospitals with female staff. During the war it soon became evident that a small number of these women, who were part of a professional elite in nursing circles, and who coped admirably with keeping order in military hospitals in peacetime, did not possess the skills to manage wartime units of up to 2000 beds, or cope with the unrelenting pressures of Casualty Clearing Stations. Some found themselves transferred back to the United Kingdom from overseas to undertake less demanding duties. More than 70 nurses who had resigned or retired from QAIMNS between 1903 and 1914, returned to serve once more, with many of the older women among them taking up positions as matrons of the smaller military hospitals in the United Kingdom, thereby releasing experienced younger matrons for service overseas. (For further details about the work of the QAIMNS, see Chapter 4.)

Queen Alexandra's Imperial Military Nursing Service Reserve

Although there had always been a small 'Reserve' of women who augmented the numbers of the regular QAIMNS, the effects of the First World War demanded that many more women needed to be recruited quickly. Trained nurses flocked to join the military nursing services on yearly contracts. By the end of 1914 more than 2200 women had enrolled in the service, and in total more than 12,000 served with the Reserve at some time during the war in all theatres.

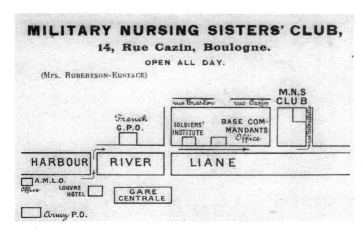

Every base town in France had a nurses' rest club. The clubs were places where nurses could read the papers, have tea and relax, or write letters. For nurses on trains or barges, they would act as a 'depot' for the British Red Cross to pick up and deliver personal laundry. Reproduced by courtesy of Sue Light.

Like their counterparts in the regular service, these women were educated, of good social standing and had all completed a three-year nurse training in a hospital approved by the War Office. They were, with very few exceptions, over 25 years of age and single, but as the war progressed a shortage of staff resulted in some married women being allowed to serve. Women were engaged on yearly contracts or until their services were no longer required, and most had been demobilised by the end of 1919, returning to civilian life to pick up the threads of their former lives, or venturing overseas to seek new opportunities.

Princess Christian's Army Nursing Service Reserve (PCANSR/ANSR)

The Army Nursing Service (ANS) was the forerunner of Queen Alexandra's Imperial Military Nursing Service. When QAIMNS's own Reserve was formed in 1908, members of the PCANSR ceased to be employed in military hospitals. Yet in September 1914 there were still 337 names on the roll, and a number of these women mobilised, wearing the uniform of the QAIMNS Reserve, but still officially part of the PCANSR. During the course of the war all mobilised members signed contracts to serve as members of Queen Alexandra's Imperial Military Nursing Service Reserve, thus erasing the final traces of Princess Christian's own nursing service.

Territorial Force Nursing Service (TFNS)

The Territorial Force Nursing Service was established by R B Haldane, the Secretary of State for War, in March 1908 following the Territorial and Reserve Forces Act (1907), and was intended to provide nursing staff for the 23 territorial force general hospitals planned for the United Kingdom in the event of war. It created a force of 2760 nurses, who in peacetime went about

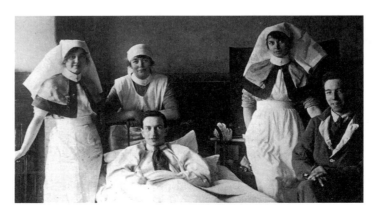

Two Territorial Force Nursing Service trained nurses, one VAD and two patients. Unsigned postcard. Reproduced by courtesy of Sue Light.

Garrould's

FOR ALL KINDS OF

NURSES' UNIFORMS	CAPS
APRONS GOWNS	BONNETS
COLLARS	CUFFS

— ALSO —
SURGICAL
INSTRUMENTS
— AND —
APPLIANCES
ETC.

To H.M. War Office
H.M. Colo ial Office
India Office
London County
Council
Metropolitan Asylums
Bo rd, etc.

Contractors to the St.
John Ambulance As-
sociation and the British
Red Cross Society.

Write for Uniform Cata-
logues, officially approved,
containing illustrations and
articulars.—POST FREE.

Now Ready.—The New Edition of GARROULD'S
NURSES' CATALOGUE with over 700 Illustrations
of Nurses' Uniforms, Surgical Instruments and
Appliances, etc., post free on application.

E. & R. GARROULD, 150 to 162, Edgware Road, London, W.
Telegrams: 'Garrould, London.'   Telephones: 5320, 5321, and 6297 Paddington.

Advertisement from 'Wails of the Wounded: or, Convalescent Carollings' from the Royal Free Military Hospital Journal, 1st June 1916. Reproduced by courtesy of Cambridge University Library (Rare Books).

their normal duties in civil hospitals and private homes, but with a commitment to the War Office and holding mobilisation orders

Although originally intended for home service only, in 1913 members of the TFNS were given the opportunity to notify their intention of willingness to serve overseas if required, and the sudden need for a large number of nurses to accompany the British Expeditionary Force to France in 1914 resulted in some members proceeding overseas during the early weeks of the war. Many of the TFNS nurses who served during the war had long experience in nursing, holding positions of great responsibility in civil life. Among them were women who, on the outbreak of war, were working as assistant matrons and senior sisters in some of the United Kingdom's great institutions, and it soon became evident that many of these women coped admirably with the management of large hospitals and female staffs. They quickly adapted their skills to meet the new and complex needs of Casualty Clearing Stations and stationary hospitals, becoming some of the war's most able nurse-managers. Over the course of the war, 8140 women served at some time as mobilised members of the Territorial Force Nursing Service, and of these 2280 served overseas.

Civil Hospital Reserve (CHR)

In 1911, the Civil Hospital Reserve was formed, to supplement the nursing services in the military hospitals in the event of war. Some of the largest of the United Kingdom's hospitals invited their trained nursing staff to offer their services to the War Office, and a register was drawn up of suitably qualified women who were willing to mobilise on the outbreak of hostilities, on the understanding that their jobs would be protected, and they would be able to return to their former roles at the end of the war. In August 1914, 600 women were ready for mobilisation with the Civil Hospital Reserve. Although they were originally intended for service in home hospitals only, many soon found themselves serving with the British Expeditionary Force in France and Flanders, and wearing the uniform of the QAIMNS Reserve.

Assistant Nurses

Before 1919 there was no register of nurses, or national regulations covering standards for nurse training. During the last two decades of the nineteenth century the realisation had dawned that a longer period of training was necessary to produce a 'professional' nurse. However, hospitals were not compelled to train nurses for three years, with the result that nursing became a two-tier system, with those who had completed three years' training in a general hospital often regarded as 'proper' nurses, while others, including women trained in fever nursing, the care of children and the mentally ill, were sometimes seen as professionally less qualified. By early 1915 applications were accepted from women who held certificates showing that they had completed an approved two-year training in fever, children's or mental nursing, or were certified midwives. Assistant nurses were not numerous, but their specialised experience proved particularly useful in the nursing of patients with infectious diseases and mental illness, and in the care of the civilian population and refugees abroad.

Long ago in the Mess I said to my Sister, laughing: 'I would go through the four years' training just to wear that cap and cape!' And she: 'You couldn't go through it and come out as you are…' —Enid Bagnold, VAD nurse, author of *A Diary Without Dates*

VADs (Members of Voluntary Aid Detachments)

On the 16th August 1909 the War Office issued its 'Scheme for the Organisation of Voluntary Aid in England and Wales'. This set up both male and female Voluntary Aid Detachments to fill certain gaps in the territorial medical services, with a similar scheme for Scotland following in December 1909. Detachments had to meet at least once a month, with many meeting as often as weekly, and women worked towards gaining certificates in Home Nursing and First Aid within twelve months of joining, learning to bandage and to do simple dressings, as well as the basics of invalid cookery and hygiene. In some areas it was arranged for them to go into local hospitals for a few hours each week to gain an insight into ward work, and due to the low number of men being recruited in certain places, women could also gain experience in outdoor activities, stretcher duties, the transport of the sick and wounded, and improvisation with whatever came to hand.

A group of VADs from No 74 General Hospital. This was open in Trouville between March 1918 and March 1919. Reproduced by courtesy of Sue Light.

Detachments were organised for their local Territorial Force Association by the Red Cross and received their training from the St John Ambulance Association. After October 1914 the detachments were run by the Joint War Committee of the British Red Cross Society and St John of Jerusalem, a wartime amalgamation. The detachments were initially intended for home service only, to staff auxiliary hospitals and rest stations, and they received no payment or salary for these duties—all the women would have been in a position, at least initially, to give their services for free.

The women who joined were a mixture, being a wide range of ages and with different sorts of life skills. As a group they were very much defined by being middle- or upper-middle class—in the main they were the daughters of local gentry, landowners, army officers, clergy, and professional men—and also included a good sprinkling of women with an aristocratic background. The majority were young women who had never had any paid employment, and of those who eventually went on to wartime service more than three-quarters had either never worked outside the home, or had done work which qualified them only for payment of a minor nature. Following the outbreak of war, members of female detachments staffed VAD hospitals and auxiliary units, and individual members quickly came to be referred to by the initials of their organisation, although they were also sometimes known as 'Red Cross nurses'. As well as nursing, they cleaned, scrubbed and dusted, set trays, cooked breakfasts; they lit fires and boiled up coppers full of washing. They also helped to dress, undress and wash the men—which was of course a big step for young women who might never have been alone and unchaperoned with a member of the opposite sex before, other than their brothers.

Since the 'Sister Dora' cap is taboo, and we have the handkerchief cap with which to tie up our head, one VAD has cut her hair short in the fashion of the bob-crop of American children. She quite rightly argues long hair to be an unnecessary waste of time and energy, unnecessary since her head must never now be uncovered except in her own bunk. One called her a wise Virgin, but we others contented ourselves by dubbing her a strong-minded female, the while conservatively and foolishly retaining our own questionable crowning-glories. —Olive Dent, VAD nurse, author of *A VAD in France*

The instructional booklet for VADs gives some hints of how these women's sheltered lives might further change: they are advised to 'Comb the hair with a small tooth comb once a day' and also instructed that 'Great care should be taken to have no hangnails or scratches on the hands. If the skin is broken, however slightly, it should be covered with gauze and collodion before assisting at an operation or doing a dressing. Carelessness in this respect may lead to blood-poisoning.' The booklet also offered a high moral tone, with an inspirational message written for them by their Commander-in-Chief including the words: 'It will be your duty not only to set an example of discipline and perfect steadiness of character, but also to maintain the most courteous relations with those whom you are helping in this great struggle.'

Red Cross VAD uniform consisted of mid-blue dresses, with white aprons, white cuffs and collars, a white cap and a white apron with a red cross embroidered on it. VADs who were part of the Order of St John, around

A NIGHT BIRD

It was extremely difficult to keep clean and dry in a field hospital. Many nurses added waterproof layers to their uniforms to protect them from rain and mud. Illustration by R M Savage 'and others', Olive Dent's A VAD in France, 1917.

a quarter of the total number, wore grey dresses with a St John armband, and no red cross on their aprons. The cap was initially a small headpiece, but by early 1915, some laxity had developed over the style of cap worn by VADs, with quite a few adopting the triangular floating 'veil' of the trained military nurse. In an effort to placate professional nurses, some of whom were already unhappy at having to work alongside the 'amateur' in wartime, the Joint War Committee introduced a new type of cap for VADs to make them easily distinguishable when in uniform: the handkerchief caps tied at the nape of the neck, a style that became so strongly associated with the First World War VAD. In the spring of 1915 the War Office agreed that VADs could be employed in the large military hospitals at home to augment the trained staff, and by early summer of that year in general hospitals overseas as well. During the course of the war more than 90,000 women served as VADs in some capacity; 10,000 worked in hospitals under the direction of the War Office, and of those 8000 served overseas, in France, Malta, Serbia, Salonika, Egypt and Mesopotamia.

Special Military Probationers (SMP)

Special Military Probationers were women who had little or no formal training as nurses. They served under almost identical conditions of service to members of Voluntary Aid Detachments and did similar work. However, these women were recruited and employed by the War Office, and had no ties with the Joint War Committee of the British Red Cross Society and St John of Jerusalem.

These eight groups of women combined to form a highly trained and professional body which, for more than five years, met the nursing needs of the British Expeditionary Force, its Allies, its prisoners of war and at times the civilian population abroad. At a time when trained nurses were in short supply, the British military nursing services never wavered in their commitment to provide the best possible nursing care to sick and wounded soldiers, in conditions unknown to them before the war. When peace was won, women who had gained independence during the war years sometimes struggled to return to their previous lives. Many continued to nurse traumatised and maimed soldiers who needed constant care, but the majority of the voluntary nurses were expected to abandon nursing for marriage, despite the catastrophic death toll meaning that there was a shortage of potential partners. Some women found themselves in limbo, unable to return to the life they had envisioned before war broke out, yet incapable of moving forward. Perhaps the inner strength that the nurses found in the horror of the Casualty Clearing Stations and the field hospitals helped them to return to a post-war world that would never be the same again.

4

'The Elite'
Queen Alexandra's Imperial Military
Nursing Service in the First World War

Eric Gruber von Arni

'The Elite' was the nickname bestowed upon serving sisters of Queen Alexandra's Imperial Military Nursing Service (QAIMNS), their Reserves, and the Territorial Force Nursing Service (TFNS), by other nurses, and members of the Voluntary Aid Detachments (VADs) working alongside them. Did the name perhaps reflect jealousy or a manifestation of subordination? For whatever reason the name stuck and throughout this chapter it is this group of professional military nurses to whom I shall refer.

Who were these nurses? Their origins came from the Army Nursing Service (ANS), a small body of nurses formed after the experiences of the Crimean and Zulu wars. In 1882, the War Office, facing the onset of yet another war, this time in the Sudan, finally accepted that the army required nurses who would operate within the over-arching structure of the army's medical services. Many of the ANS sisters were recruited from London hospitals, particularly the London Hospital, Whitechapel. However, it was soon recognised that there would be a problem should Great Britain become embroiled in a

Nurses waiting to board a hospital train. Reproduced by courtesy of Army Medical Services Museum.

major European war crisis, as the ANS was not structured in a way that would allow it to expand rapidly to supply future needs.

In January 1901, the Princess of Wales, later to become Queen Alexandra, organised the dispatch of nurses of the ANS to the Boer War. Upon their return to England, those who had rendered outstanding service in South Africa were personally presented with a badge by Queen Alexandra who took a particular interest in their work. The Queen continued to have a direct influence on army nursing and in 1902 Queen Alexandra's Imperial Military Nursing Service was formed to provide a body of professional nurses specially selected for employment in military hospitals. Later, in 1904, came the introduction of a large QAIMNS Reserve for mobilisation in war. Although the sisters did not hold an army rank, they were afforded officer status, and their organisation came under the direct patronage of Queen Alexandra who took an active role in their formation and work.

Far down the corridor a slim figure in white approaches, dwarfed by the smoky distance; her nun-like cap floating, her scarlet cape, the 'cape of pride,' slipped round her narrow shoulders. How intent and silent They are! I watched this one pass with a look half-reverence, half-envy. One should never aspire to know a Sister intimately. They are disappointing people; without candour, without imagination. Yet what a look of personality hangs about them... —Enid Bagnold, VAD nurse, author of *A Diary Without Dates*

Very quickly, serving QAIMNS sisters were to be found working around the world: in China during the Boxer Rebellion, in Africa and also in a special Indian branch of the service. Their work demanded an ability to rough it whilst nursing in very difficult and often unsuitable circumstances and they swiftly learned to cope in a variety of trying conditions. Their adaptability together with a familiarity with the military gained over many years of service produced a body of nurses admirably equipped to form the core of a military nursing service when war came. These abilities set them apart from the untrained volunteers who so bravely joined the Voluntary Aid Detachments, and who worked alongside Millicent Sutherland, learning on the job and looking towards 'the elite' to show the way.

Immediately following the declaration of war in August 1914, QAIMNS sisters, their Reserves and the recently formed TFNS were all mobilised. One member of the QAIMNS, Sister Jean Todd, who was working in the

Cambridge Military Hospital in Aldershot, has left a graphic description of her experience of mobilisation which came early in August 1914, shortly after the onset of war. After a hectic round of packing and the purchase of recommended 'war stores' she travelled quickly to Millbank in London where she met up with the other members of her new unit. Later, while she waited to board a troopship in Southampton, she wrote: 'Are we on our way to the war? I suppose we are—we have dawdled here and there waiting to embark for France but the last news was that we were not to go aboard until 7pm and oh! if only I could take off this bonnet and cape and collar and cuffs and shoes and lie flat under a tree but alas, if one is going to a war .... !'

Her unit, No 9 General Hospital, eventually established itself as a base hospital in a sports arena in Nantes. Patients started arriving before the hospital had existed 48 hours. Convoys came and went and the camp quickly settled into working order. During September they were as busy as they thought it was possible to be. Then in October the workload lessened and, at the end of the month,

" PETTICOAT LANE "

A hospital under canvas—bell tents were often used as accommodation for nurses. Illustration by R M Savage 'and others', Olive Dent's *A VAD in France,* 1917.

the hospital was packed up and moved to Rouen. There the nursing staff had their first experience of patients suffering from the effects of chlorine gas.

Chlorine gas was first used on the Western Front by the Germans on 22nd April 1915 at the start of the Second Battle of Ypres. When inhaled, this terrible toxic chemical made breathing difficult by burning casualties' air passages. Fluid filled their lungs whilst eyes, ears and throat were also affected. The large numbers of casualties from gas attacks often frequently also experienced skin burns on exposed flesh and internal organs. As the war continued, additional, even more devastating, chemical weapons were developed including phosgene and mustard gas.

Nurses moved frequently. Sister Packer recalled:

> Orders came to pack and retire. We were up and running again three days later in tents further down the line and are now crowded out with wounded. We settled down for six weeks and then moved once more, this time into huts and gardens. Wards were made homelike with chintz and shades. Wounded coming all the time and then the Spanish Flu struck and in rooms designated for twenty men, forty are lying. Life was hard. We were near a rail head and the Bosch thought fit to bomb us. On 20th July, thirty-eight bombs were dropped. We dipped our heads each time and hoped for better times. Our quarters were riddled and souvenirs lay everywhere. One sister was hit, but not badly, and at 4am we had tea and biscuits and went back to bed.

In the early stages of the war it was considered inappropriate for 'lady nurses' to be deployed in Casualty Clearing Stations as the provision of suitable accommodation would be too difficult and it was wrongly thought that there would be little need for trained nurses in what were perceived as 'little more than enlarged dressing stations'. However, as Casualty Clearing Stations became semi-permanent hospitals in October 1914 it was agreed that nurses should be permitted to work in these units, sometimes very close to the front line.

Transportation of patients posed many problems. With an almost continual arrival of sick and wounded at the forward medical units, the logistical difficulties of evacuating any patients capable of being moved were met with a variety of solutions. The modes of transportation varied according to local circumstances. For example, from the spring of 1915 until the autumn of 1918, the army operated ambulance barges on the inland waterways and canals of France and the Low Countries, carrying the sick and wounded from the Casualty Clearing Stations back to the base hospitals. Sister Millicent Peterkin QAIMNS(R) worked as a sister in charge of a hospital barge for several months in the latter stages of the war. She wrote:

Interior of a hospital barge awaiting patients. This barge has a lift to lower patients inside, located immediately behind the standing figures. Reproduced by courtesy of Army Medical Services Museum.

On these barges, the ward area was contained in the large central portion of the vessel whilst the cabins for the medical officers and the sisters, two bathrooms, a dispensary, a pack store and a store-room for linen and medical comforts were at the stern of the barge.

The forward end was occupied by cabins for the crew and orderlies, a kitchen, larder, coal bunker and a dynamo room. At this end also was the companion ladder that led through a hatchway to the deck. The actual top of the barge was somewhat rounded whilst a narrow ledge, on which it was possible for a man to stand with both feet together with only an inch or two to spare, went right around the side. This was the part on which the nurses had to walk when proceeding from one end of the barge to the other. There was no handrail, only a tiny wooden ledge about half an inch high and a drop of many feet on the outer side, and into dirty water too! However, one soon learnt to balance oneself and to walk quite smartly along the narrow ledge. In frosty weather, though, it was really dangerous and an icy bath was the usual result of a slip as several people, both sisters and men, found to their cost. More than once I have been reduced to crawling ignominiously on my hands and knees along the roof as being the only safe way of progression.

In the centre of the barge was a manually operated lift and when a load of patients was to be taken on board the hatch over the lift was removed and a broad firm gangway laid from the top of the barge to the canal bank. The barge medical officer stood on the bank beside the ambulances and directed the loading. Each stretcher was carried up the gangway, laid on the lift and lowered to the ward deck level where the corporal and nursing orderlies lifted the patient carefully onto their allocated beds. The men worked quickly and methodically and the loading was rapidly accomplished. After the patients were all in bed I went around and entered their names and other particulars in my treatment book, also the diets they were to have and any necessary treatment. At the same time the staff nurse took the patients' temperatures and pulse rates. As soon as the patients were all on board the medical officer came to see if anything was required and we would then get underway. From the patients' point of view, the barges travelled so smoothly that they scarcely ever knew when they began to move.

Going to bed is a prodigious rite and ceremony. After a bath in a camp bath, which against the feeble force of chilblained fingers has a maximum resistance, immovability and inertia, and yet seems to possess a centre of gravity more elusive than mercury, one dons pyjamas, cholera belt, pneumonia jacket, bed socks, and bed stockings as long and woolly as a Father Christmas's, and then piles on the bed travelling rug, dressing gown and fur coat. —Olive Dent, VAD nurse, author of *A VAD in France*

The barges only travelled in daylight. In wet or wintery weather the hatches were kept closed and ventilation was solely by fans and ventilators. The latter could not be opened at night if lights were burning in case of enemy aircraft attacks (nurses often sat in total darkness with only a small torch for use when working on urgent cases). Consequently the air became stiflingly hot and malodorous, especially when the barge contained patients who had been gassed. As well as the frustration of being unable to help these men, the staff often suffered from the effects of gas themselves, with sore eyes, sickness and difficulty in breathing resulting from inhaling the toxic vapours emanating from the soldiers' impregnated clothing and exhaled breath. Other hazards included broken ice damaging the hulls and frequent bombing attacks in close proximity.

Patients were also conveyed by ambulance trains under similar conditions. During the early stages of the war, these were roughly converted freight wagons with entirely unconnected carriages. Only later were passenger trains employed. If the train were in motion, the only way to move from one coach to another was by way of the external footboards, a procedure supposedly forbidden but nevertheless widely practised out of necessity, as described by Sister M Phillips QAIMNS: 'In the very early hours of a beautiful September morning in 1914, a French stationmaster in a little out-of-the-way French village probably remembered for the rest of his life the sight that met his amazed gaze when an ambulance train flew at speed through his station carrying an English nursing sister clinging like a limpet to the side of the train.'

I was falling asleep when Sister Kirby rushed into my room, calling out, 'Sister Millicent! The wounded!' I rushed down the stone stairs. The wounded, indeed! Six motor-cars and as many wagons were at the door, and they were carrying in those unhappy fellows. Some were on stretchers, others were supported by willing Red Cross men. One or two of the stragglers fell up the steps from fatigue and lay there. Many of these men had been for three days without food or sleep in the trenches. —**Millicent, Duchess of Sutherland**

In the early days, patients were entrained fully dressed with all the dirt, mud and blood of battle on them. Many of them had not had their boots off for five or six weeks and, as another nurse writes, 'Only those who have done it can know what it is to undress a heavy man, badly wounded and lying on the narrow seat of a railway carriage.' The work on ambulance trains eased somewhat following the establishment of nurses in Casualty Clearing Stations. When they were present, the men were entrained washed, fed and dressed in pyjamas.

Nurses employed in hospital ships were invariably army nurses. Sister A Meldrum, QAIMNS(R) was posted to the hospital ship *Anglia* in May 1915, frequently completing two return cross-channel journeys in one day until, 'on the 17th November, after the ship had taken about 500 patients aboard at Boulogne, at about 12 noon, some six miles out from Dover, there was a

HMHS Anglia *sinking—17th November 1915*. Reproduced by courtesy of Army Medical Services Museum.

tremendous crash with iron girders and so forth coming falling down like matchwood'. She soon realised that the ship had either been torpedoed or had struck a mine.

Her first act was to fasten a life-jacket on herself so that she would be in a better position to help others. The sisters, orderlies and the patients who were able to do so put on theirs. Walking cases were ordered on deck whilst Sister Meldrum immediately set about removing splints to prevent their weight sinking the patients as they abandoned ship. 'As many men as possible were carried up on deck where those that could threw themselves into the sea whilst others were let down in the lifeboat. Unfortunately, it was only possible to lower one boat as the ship was sinking so rapidly. Even though the majority of cases suffered from fractured limbs, severe wounds and amputations, there was no panic whatsoever.'

After Sister Meldrum had satisfied herself that there was no possible chance of getting any more patients out as the bows were quite under water, she scrambled onto the rudder. The propellers were still turning at a terrific speed, posing yet another significant danger, so she jumped into the sea where hundreds of patients were still struggling in the water. It was some time before the destroyers were able to help by lowering their lifeboats and searching for survivors. Unfortunately in her case, after a lifeboat had reached her and hauled her aboard, so many patients attempted to hang onto the sides of the vessel that it capsized. Once again the passengers were thrown into the sea. Although there were many armless and legless men struggling in the water, very many were eventually saved. Sister Meldrum was in the water for about 40 minutes before being taken on board a destroyer. Later, when writing her memoirs, she quipped: 'Forty minutes in the Channel in November is not the kind of sea-bathing that one would indulge in from choice!'

Sister E M Carter, a Reserve QAIMNS sister, spent extended periods of service aboard the hospital ship HMHS *Asturias* which plied between Southampton, the Dardanelles and Alexandria. When the *Asturias* neared the Dardanelles peninsula, she could hear the guns and see the shells bursting as she witnessed the latest unsuccessful attempt to capture an objective on the Gallipoli Peninsula. She wrote:

12th July: Much nearer to land now. Nearly went over a mine when moving. It was exploded while we were at breakfast. A battleship is bombarding the entrance to the Dardanelles. We are expecting a very busy day receiving patients. 11pm: I feel it's too much to attempt to describe today. The wounded have been coming on all day. About 200 on board now, some most terribly ill, some dying, one died this afternoon. Dozens of haemorrhage cases. The fighting really has been fierce and the slaughter truly fearful. The wounded are still being shipped and it's nearly midnight.

13th July: We did not finish dressings until 10.00pm and then worked until 12.00 midnight in theatre which is still going. The firing has ceased a little but I can hear the barges still at their grievous work. The fighting continued all night with the wounded being shipped continuously and the theatre going throughout. We have been doing dressings all day, scarcely stopping for meals. A queue has been waiting the whole of the time and it seems we should never get to the end of it. As a matter of fact, we didn't even though three sisters came down after dinner to help us out. The next day we even found some whose wounds had been missed.

They finally finished at 11.45pm with some 400 beds in the steerage ward and four nurses doing 100 dressings each. Instead of the standard 1000 patients maximum, 1600 soldiers were taken on board. Men were brought in straight from the trenches, mostly covered with earth and sand. As HMHS *Asturias* left the peninsula at 5am on 14th July heading for Alexandria, Sister Carter mused that 'time has passed like five years instead of just the one week since arriving at the Dardanelles'.

At the start of the war in August 1914, there were just 300 trained nurses serving in the QAIMNS (matrons, sisters and staff nurses). Additionally, some 200 QAIMNS Reserves and 600 nurses earmarked from Civil Hospitals and the TFNS were available to be called up for service alongside the QAIMNS on the outbreak of war. As the war progressed, the numbers of nurses enrolled into the QAIMNS rose until, at war's end, a total of 10,404 nurses had served at home and abroad. The First World War saw nurses of the QAIMNS, their Reserves and the TFNS posted into nearly every sphere of conflict, including France and Flanders, Italy, Mesopotamia, Salonika, Russia and East Africa. Even after the 1918 Armistice the requirement for medical and nursing staff on the continent did not end and forward medical units continued to advance with the troops into Germany providing care for both servicemen and local civilians.

Regrettably, not all nurses made it home. Some 26 members of the QAIMNS, its Reserves and the TFNS were either killed or drowned through enemy action whilst another nine were killed in the many types of accidents common in wartime. In total 141 died while serving, 71 abroad and 70 at home from a variety of causes, including the pandemic influenza, as well as other illnesses common in times of war such as cholera and typhus.

Perhaps the attitudes of relief and occasional periods of relaxation available to those nurses still serving in France and Flanders after the Armistice may be summed up by allowing the last words in this chapter to fall to a QAIMNS matron working in Calais in December and January 1918:

> This was a very happy time for us all. Imperial nurses were not allowed then to dance at all, either in their own mess or away. Meanwhile, Canadian, South African and American nurses had dances every week, and we felt we must do something about it, for this occasion at least. Permission was asked from

the War Office and consent was given for us to dance from Christmas till New Year's Day, both days inclusive. This permission did not reach us, however, until 27 December so we had already lost three days and had to make the most of what was left. There were great preparations for the festivity. Up at 35 General Hospital there was to be a big affair, but I only had a little place and could not accept more than fifteen couples. But we did quite well. We had two empty wards and one sitting room. One I used as a buffet with nice refreshments: ham, beef and sardine sandwiches, trifle, Dundee cake from England, grapes, apples from the Canadian Red Cross, coffee, Bovril, hot milk and a little wine. Officers from the Canadian Air Force came as well as old friends from the staff of the Prisoners of War Camp. The Canadians were especially fine dancers and taught us two new ones, the hesitation waltz and one other. We danced the Lancers too. I was glad to see that my VADs and the men were also having a real Christmas party. I heard afterwards that mine was the nicest dance in the area as everybody had enough to eat. Some who came back from 35 General were very cross and hungry, as the refreshments there did not go around.

Perhaps the nickname 'The Elite' was not too far short of the mark!

Oil painting 1 by Victor Tardieu, August, 1915: Millicent, Duchess of Sutherland, Attending to her Patients. Tardieu's admiration of Millicent Sutherland and her work at the hospital is evident in this painting. She is shown to be in complete control of both herself and her domain. Reproduced by courtesy of Abbott & Holder JV.

Oil painting 2 by Victor Tardieu, 1915: Tents with Stores and Flower Tub. Stores and beds have been dragged outside, perhaps in preparation for new arrivals from the front. Tent flaps have been rolled aside for ventilation. Reproduced by courtesy of Abbott & Holder JV.

Oil painting 3 by Victor Tardieu, 1915: Patient with Head Injury and Seated Man with Uniform Cap. The great coat hanging from a central tent pole and the proximity of the beds gives an impression of how cramped the nurses' working conditions were, despite the idyllic fields outside. Reproduced by courtesy of Abbott & Holder JV.

Oil painting 4 by Victor Tardieu, August, 1915: Unfinished Work—The Artist Astride a Stool. Tardieu's oil paintings of the camp in the oatfield were a personal response to his experiences at Bourbourg. Reproduced by courtesy of Abbott & Holder JV.

Oil painting 5 by Victor Tardieu, August, 1915: Two Men Propped up in Bed, Posing for the Artist. Patient notes can be seen hanging from the pole above each bed, showing the ingenuity of the nurses in their improvised hospital. Reproduced by courtesy of Abbott & Holder JV.

Oil painting 6 by Victor Tardieu, 1915: Two Soldiers Propped up in Iron Beds. The colourful bedspreads and jaunty striped awnings borrowed from nearby seafront hotels provided a cheerful atmosphere to ameliorate the suffering of the wounded. Reproduced by courtesy of Abbott & Holder JV.

Oil painting 7 by Victor Tardieu, September, 1915: View from Tent of Patients Convalescing in Deckchairs. Tardieu emphasises the healing environment created by the nurses, helping the men recuperate from the horrors of the front line. Reproduced by courtesy of Abbott & Holder JV.

Oil painting 8 by Victor Tardieu, 1915: Soldier with Arm in Sling, Seated on a Camp Bed with a Fellow Patient. Although the scenes painted by Tardieu show a bright sunny and peaceful hospital, noise from the fighting along the nearby front line would have ensured that patients and medical staff were always aware of the war. Reproduced by courtesy of Abbott & Holder JV.

Oil painting 9 by Victor Tardieu, 1915: Soldier on an Iron Bed, Facing his Comrades. Tardieu shows the sunlight pouring though the canvas in subtle shades of lavender, pink and green as a result of the camouflage painted on the exterior due to the threat of air attacks. Reproduced by courtesy of Abbott & Holder JV.

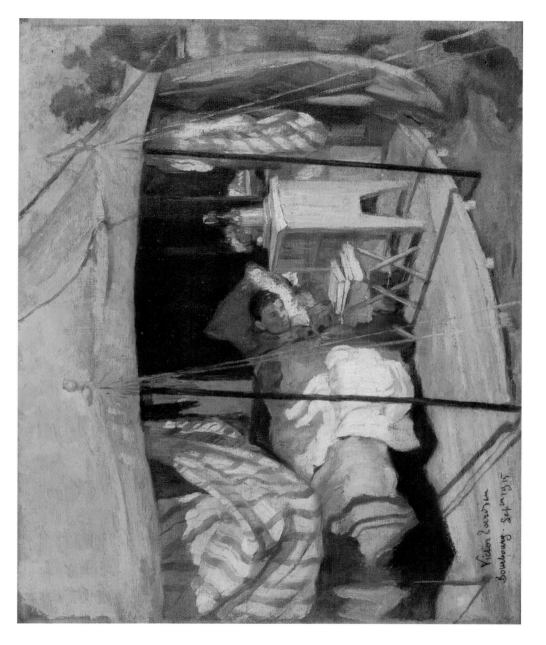

Oil painting 10 by Victor Tardieu September, 1915: Boy Asleep in a Tent. The red shawl across the boy's shoulders highlights his flushed face, emphasised by Tardieu's use of viridian green for the pillow. The awnings are raised to allow fresh air and sunshine to aid recovery. Reproduced by courtesy of Abbott & Holder JV.

Oil painting by Ellis Roberts: Millicent, Duchess of Sutherland. *The Duchess's beauty and dignity is perfectly captured in this portrait. The book she holds in her right hand indicates her love of writing.* Reproduced by courtesy of The Sutherland Dunrobin Trust.

Helen Jordan's work uniform, 1916. Youth and function is displayed in this modern style. The apron is heavily starched cotton with machine-embroidered Red Cross appliqué and has mother-of-pearl buttons and metal closures. Reproduced by courtesy of Harvard Medical School Archives Collection.

Helen Jordan's work uniform, 1916, showing armband made of cotton with machine-sewn hems. Chain-stitch red embroidery features H U signifying 'Harvard Unit'.

'I wore H. U. band on sleeve and everyone looked at it with such an interested, questioning expression.'

Reproduced by courtesy of Harvard Medical School Archives Collection.

Helen Jordan's dress uniform, 1916. The thigh-length cape has a fashionable raised-collar style. The long skirt has a cummerbund style waistband and straps crisscrossed over the front bodice for functional stability. Label: H J Nicoll & Co Ltd. Reproduced by courtesy of Harvard Medical School Archives Collection.

Detail of Helen Jordan's dress uniform, 1916. Reproduced by courtesy of Harvard Medical School Archives Collection.

Helen Jordan's work dress: long-sleeved, cuffed, and including metal hook and eye closures. This garment was probably purchased at Harrods in London, 1916. Reproduced by courtesy of Harvard Medical School Archives Collection.

Woman's day dress, 1915. Made from light wool and lace with double-layer sleeves and lace yoke. This outfit has a clear connection to youth and function in much the same way that uniforms for nurses did from this period. The blue-and-white colour palette is found in many uniforms. Reproduced by courtesy of Harvard Medical School Archives Collection.

*At the outbreak of war, thousands of women volunteered to nurse
the wounded, being posted to both hospitals in Britain and abroad.
Recruitment poster for the Voluntary Aid Detachment, 1914-1918.
Designed by Joyce Dennys.* Reproduced by courtesy of the
British Red Cross Museum and Archives.

The Spanish influenza pandemic of 1918-19 was responsible for millions of deaths worldwide, and is particularly noteworthy for the unusually high numbers of deaths among the previously young and healthy. This international post-war tragedy is often overshadowed by the horrors of the First World War. Danse Macabre by Robert Harrison is a modern interpretation of the 1918 influenza, unusually depicting Death as a governess or nursemaid. Reproduced by courtesy of Robert Harrison.

5

Traumas of Conflict
Nursing the Wounded of the First World War

•◆•

Christine Hallett

The women who cared for the sick and wounded of the First World War came from a range of backgrounds. Some were fully qualified professional nurses with two or three years' training from a recognised school; others were volunteers with just a handful of training certificates and only a few months' experience of hospital work. Together, in military hospitals at home and overseas, they worked to save the lives and restore the health of men damaged by war. On the Western Front, in the eastern Mediterranean and on more distant war fronts, nurses and volunteers, along with military orderlies, cared for patients with some of the most horrific war wounds that had ever been seen. They also supported men with severe life-threatening illnesses such as typhus fever, dysentery, malaria and, at the end of the war, the highly virulent Spanish influenza. In an era before antibiotics, the careful and diligent nursing of often desperately sick patients meant the difference between life and death. But by working to protect the lives and health of severely traumatised men, in sometimes highly dangerous environments, nurses and volunteers exposed themselves to risk, exhaustion and emotional distress. Although a few of the professional nurses who undertook wartime nursing already had military experience, and others

The man who received extreme unction the night before is mad with terror. I do not believe he is after all so badly wounded. He has a bullet in his shoulder, and it is not serious. He has lost all power of speech, but I believe that he is example of what I have read of and what I had never seen—a man dying of sheer fright. —**Millicent, Duchess of Sutherland**

were quite 'battle-hardened' by their encounters with trauma and disease in civilian hospitals, other more newly qualified nurses, along with the tens of

Two nurses outside their tent, Bourbourg camp, 1915. Photographer: Oswald Gayer Morgan. Reproduced by courtesy of Louise and Robert Skioldebrand.

thousands of volunteer nurses who assisted them, were totally unprepared for the horrors of the First World War military hospital. It is almost impossible for us to imagine just how shocking an experience nursing work must have been for many of these young women.

The Trauma of War-service

When Millicent, Duchess of Sutherland wrote about her experiences in war-torn Belgium in 1914, she described how she 'felt stunned—as if I were passing through an endless nightmare'. As has already been described in Chapter 1, she had led a hospital unit to Belgium soon after Britain's declaration of war on Germany in August 1914, and had established a field hospital in a convent in Namur, caring for the wounded of the shattered Belgian army. The injuries she encountered were beyond anything she had ever imagined. The First World War was Europe's first encounter with industrial warfare at close quarters: the blast injuries caused by shrapnel-shells could destroy limbs, create deep holes in men's bodies, or leave them with huge areas of lacerated flesh. Burns could be extensive and severe. Nor were distressing injuries the only traumas that nurses had to face. While Millicent and her unit were in Namur, much of the town was burned to the ground, and she and her staff were taken prisoner by the German army, before being escorted on foot to the Dutch border, where they were released.

Other Belgian units fared equally badly. Mabel St Clair Stobart's Women's Sick and Wounded Convoy Corps was also overrun by the German advance, and Stobart herself was almost shot as a spy before persuading the German commander who had taken her prisoner that her work was purely humanitarian. One anonymous nurse-memoirist wrote of how her volunteer unit had been subjected to bombardment in Antwerp, before being evacuated by bus to Ostend. On the fourteen-hour journey to the coast, she sat alongside a patient with several broken ribs, using her arm as a splint. Opposite her sat two men, each with a fractured leg propped up on her knees.

In Serbia, in 1915, several volunteer units were once again faced with the options of flight or imprisonment, as a joint German-Bulgarian force entered the country, pushing thousands of troops and refugees south and west towards the Albanian Alps. Several hospital units joined their flight to the Adriatic, climbing thousands of feet to the high mountain passes that led to safety. The month was December and paths were often deep with snow or slippery with ice. En route, nurses passed the bodies of those who had died of starvation or exposure, and at night they slept in hay-sheds or alpine shelters. Those who remained behind were taken prisoner and were put to work in squalid and sometimes typhus-infested hospitals for several months, caring for Serbian soldier-prisoners, before being escorted to the Swiss border and released.

About noon the rain comes, sending us all on duty after lunch, fully armed against its torrential attentions—two pairs of stockings, gum boots, shortest dress, belted mackintosh, together with sou'wester in place of, or over, our cap, since diving in and out of dripping tents soon gives one's stiffest starchiest cap the appearance of a time-worn dish rag. —**Olive Dent, VAD nurse, author of** *A VAD in France*

In the Aegean Sea, during and after the Gallipoli campaign, hospital ships were in constant danger, as they moved between the peninsula, the island of Lemnos and bases in Egypt and Malta. Although hospital ships were never deliberately targeted by German submarine commanders, some were accidentally torpedoed or were sunk by mines. In October 1915, the

A " BAIRNSPATHER BUNK "

Interior of a nurse's accommodation hut. Nurses and other medical staff became adept at improvising to create a home-like atmosphere in their tents and huts. Illustration by R M Savage 'and others' Olive Dent's A VAD in France, 1917.

troopship *Marquette*, transporting 36 members of the New Zealand Army Nursing Service to Salonika as part of a hospital unit was torpedoed, and sank within fifteen minutes. Ten nurses died of injury or exposure, and some of those who survived were severely physically and emotionally damaged.

Some of the most severely traumatised nurses were those based in Casualty Clearing Stations on the Western Front. Alice Fitzgerald, an American nurse who worked with the British nursing services in France, served in a Casualty Clearing Station at Méaulte within eight miles of the front lines. She described how in 1916 during the Battle of the Somme, her fear of shrapnel-injury was so acute that she slept in her bell-tent at night with a steel helmet over her face.

Her fear was well-founded. British nurse Nellie Spindler was killed on 22nd August 1917 at a Casualty Clearing Station near Brandhoek, when a piece of shrapnel from a bursting shell tore through the canvas of her tent and entered her chest. From 1917 onwards, bases on the French coast were frequently subjected to aerial bombardment. On 19th May, 1918, three Canadian nurses were killed and five wounded when their base hospital at Étaples was subjected to a direct hit from the air.

The Trauma of Witnessing

When historian Peter Liddle interviewed British volunteer nurse Florence Farmborough in 1975 about her wartime experiences with the Russian Red Cross he asked her what it was like to nurse severely injured Russian soldiers.

She responded that the one thing she had feared the most on first entering war service had been that she would be unable to view a dead body without being overcome by emotion. But, she commented sadly, witnessing death soon became a commonplace experience. In the course of the war, she was present at literally hundreds of deaths—some peaceful, others filled with pain and trauma. Death became a commonplace experience for all who worked in military hospitals; but some deaths were worse than others. In Casualty Clearing Stations dying patients were cared for in moribund wards. In base hospitals, dying soldiers were usually 'specialled': screens were placed around the patient's bed, and a nurse would be released from her normal duties to stay with him and keep him pain-free and comfortable. Her off-duty hours were restricted and her world became confined to the narrow space behind the screens. The worst cases were patients with septic injuries, who suffered intense pain. Tetanus patients had to be kept calm, quiet and pain-free; any sudden noise or movement would send their entire bodies into spasm. Their backs would arch, and their mouths would be forced into a macabre and horribly painful rictus grin. Very few such patients survived.

Yet nurses had the comfort of knowing that 'specialled' patients had received all possible care and attention. The greatest personal traumas came when nurses were faced with 'rushes' of patients. During large assaults on the Western Front, Casualty Clearing Stations and base hospitals were inundated with casualties. 'What is nursing here?' asked Alice Fitzgerald, as she knelt in the mud of her ward at her Casualty Clearing Station, able to give only the most cursory attention to each of hundreds of severely damaged patients. Such working conditions were an affront to the highly trained professionals of the military nursing services, who had been prepared to offer meticulous fundamental care and to mobilise their carefully honed technical skills to save life and offer comfort. One nurse in

After days of continuous heavy duty and scamped, inadequate meals, our nerves were none too reliable, and I don't suppose I was the only member of the staff whose teeth chattered with sheer terror as we groped our way to our individual huts in response to the order to scatter. One young Sister, who had previously been shelled at a Casualty Clearing Station, lost her nerve and rushed screaming through the Mess, two others seized her and held her down while the raid lasted to prevent her causing a panic. —Vera Brittain, VAD nurse, author of *Testament of Youth*

NOCTURNAL INTRUDERS

An invasion of rats into a field hospital was a not uncommon occurrence. Illustration by R M Savage 'and others', Olive Dent's *A VAD in France*, 1917.

charge of a ward at a Casualty Clearing Station, who received 45 dangerously ill patients in one night, fifteen of whom died before morning, broke down physically and emotionally, and had to be admitted to the Princess Louise's Convalescent Home at Hardelot.

The Trauma of Nursing Work

Early twentieth-century nursing was labour intensive. In an era in which the significance of infective microorganisms was well researched, but antibiotics had not yet been discovered, nurses were responsible for ward cleaning, patient hygiene, the antiseptic treatment of wounds, and the safeguarding of aseptic surgical procedures. In a Casualty Clearing Station or base hospital, the fundamental care of patients took on a new dimension. Severely wounded men arrived at military hospitals still caked in the mud of the trenches. The work of removing this filth was described by one nurse as a 'task worthy of Hercules'. But filthy, infected wounds had to be treated with the same meticulous care and attention as an aseptic surgical incision. Antiseptics were used liberally, and nurses were deeply involved in the development of wound-irrigation processes, such as the Carrel-Dakin technique, which was pioneered at Compiègne (see page 8 for a description). Such techniques were exhausting to implement: not only did nurses prepare the Dakins solution, they also washed and sterilised the complex array of glass and rubber tubing through which it was delivered into the deepest and most infected parts of patients' wounds.

Cover of a booklet published to mark the closing of No 2 General Hospital, Le Havre in the spring of 1919.

The mutilating injuries of the First World War presented nurses with sometimes insurmountable challenges, but emotional trauma— referred to as shell shock—could place them at physical risk too. Patients would wake suddenly from sleep, still engulfed in the horror of their nightmares, and nurses learned to approach them with caution at such times to avoid physical assault.

Among the most onerous duties was the care of gassed patients. Toxic gases such as chlorine and phosgene made it almost impossible for patients to breathe, and nurses had to reposition helpless patients frequently, to permit the drainage of secretions from partially destroyed lungs. Gas-damaged eyes required two-hourly irrigation with sodium bicarbonate, and nurses often found that they had only just completed one round of eye irrigations when another was required. When mustard gas was introduced in 1917, the care of patients became even more difficult and emotionally draining, because eye and lung damage was accompanied by severe blistering chemical burns which had to be dressed.

During the second decade of the twentieth century, nursing work, even in the apparently safe environment of a civilian hospital, was dangerous. Fundamental care—the lifting, bathing, turning, supporting and toileting of weak or helpless patients— was heavy and onerous, while the exposure to infective microorganisms, and other dangerous substances such as toxic disinfectant chemicals and X-rays, meant that nurses were constantly at risk. In wartime scenarios, these dangers were multiplied and nurses were exposed to many different forms of trauma. They experienced the hardships of war service: life in a tented or hutted hospital, where hours of duty could be long and conditions primitive; the dangers posed by the movements of opposing forces, which sometimes meant that they were obliged to undertake hazardous journeys, or were captured and held as prisoners-of-war; and the immediate threat to life posed by bombardment on land and torpedoing at sea. They also experienced the emotional trauma of caring for injured patients many of whom were so severely mutilated that they were almost unrecognisable as human beings; and the enervating work of remaining morally strong enough to support men with deep emotional and spiritual, as well as physical, wounds. Above all, they struggled with the trauma of nursing work itself: the care of men who arrived in Casualty Clearing Stations or base hospitals with the mud of the trenches clinging to their bodies and uniforms, debilitated by exposure and lack of adequate food, and often infested with lice; the technically demanding work of wound care; and the treatment of damage caused by toxic gases.

First World War nursing was complex and challenging work, which sometimes took place under dangerous conditions. Although the trauma to which they were exposed was nothing like as intense as that experienced by their patients, and although most recovered quickly from their war service, some nurses suffered acute physical and emotional distress. A few obtained compensation, in the form of a war pension, but others struggled, unsupported, with chronic illness for the rest of their lives. Many wrote of being 'haunted' by their experiences, and were dismayed by the idea that began to emerge in the 1920s that the war had been nothing more than a futile waste of life. Some wrote of their pride that not only had they been such a significant part of the war effort, they had also experienced at close quarters the realities of what their patients had endured. This understanding would carry them through the challenges of the post-war years, and would enable them to develop further both the clinical expertise and the professionalism which the rigours of war service had helped to mould.

6

Ten Paintings of the Hospital in the Oatfield by Victor Tardieu (1915)

•◆•

Danuta Kneebone

Victor Tardieu painting at the Bourbourg Field Hospital 1915. Photographer: Oswald Gayer Morgan. Reproduced by courtesy of Louise and Robert Skioldebrand.

A striking record of the tented field hospital at Bourbourg was created by the French artist Victor Tardieu in 1915. The Millicent Sutherland Ambulance camp was at Bourbourg for less than five months, and but for these works its existence might have been overlooked among many such histories and transitions. Tardieu's vignettes provide a vivid and colourful record of the place, its people and the time.

At the outbreak of war, Victor Tardieu (1870-1937) was an established artist in France with a successful practice in portraits, industrial and decorative scenes, and large public murals. Tardieu's family were silk merchants from a small town outside Lyons. He trained at the Écoles de Beaux-

Arts in both Lyons and Paris, going on to produce designs for stained-glass windows in public buildings and churches. Tardieu regularly exhibited at the Société des Artistes Français, and in 1902 won the *Prix National* for a vast painting, entitled *Travail (Work)*, spanning over eighteen square meters, which depicted workmen on a construction site. This two-year travel award allowed him to visit the port cities of London, Liverpool and Genoa, where he painted working men against the backdrop of docklands. Over time, Tardieu's painting style became less academic and more naturalistic, adapting Impressionist and Post-Impressionist techniques to his purpose. This can be seen in his smaller scale decorative and domestic pieces. In these pictures Tardieu allowed himself considerably more freedom in experimentation and style than in his official works, showing how he was influenced by Nabism and Fauve colouration. In these smaller-scale works, Tardieu contrasts bright sunshine with modulated colours in shadows and shade, producing some of his most innovative and colourful paintings—a technique which he subsequently used in his paintings of the field hospital.

At the outbreak of war in 1914 Tardieu was 45, too old to be called up. Nevertheless, he enlisted in the French army as a soldier. He was posted to the front as a liaison officer to the AFS (American Field Service), also known under its French title SSA (*Section Sanitaire Americaine*). This voluntary ambulance unit assisted with the transportation of wounded men from the front line to field hospitals. The hospital organised and run by the Millicent Sutherland Ambulance was under the control of the French authorities from its arrival in France. Photographs survive of ambulance trucks with both 'AFS' and 'Millicent Sutherland Ambulance' painted on their sides, demonstrating the joint logistics of these units coordinating evacuation of the wounded. Clearly the AFS was working with the Bourbourg field hospital, if not stationed at the

The first day's duty in a camp hospital is a perplexing, nonplussing affair. Primarily, I wasn't certain where I was. For a bird's eye view of the camp would have revealed a forest of marquees and a webbing of tent ropes. The marquees sometimes clustered so close that the ropes of two roofs on the adjoining side were not pegged to the ground, but were tied overhead, the one to the other, so supporting each other and saving space. Between such dual marquees was a tarpaulin passage, usually spoken of as a tunnel.
—Olive Dent, VAD nurse, author of *A VAD in France*

hospital itself, and this helps explain Tardieu's presence at this voluntary hospital. No official war artists were commissioned in France at this time, so Tardieu's paintings are probably his personal responses to the circumstances he found at the tented field hospital at Bourbourg.

The paintings of the camp are oils on wooden panels, more like compositional sketches or loose preparatory works than finished pieces. Tardieu has a broad expressive handling of paint, with sweeping brush strokes, masses of light and shade, and contrasting bright colours. The paintings seem to capture the spontaneity of the artist's first inspirational ideas, rather than being worked and reworked. The small wood panels, possibly of cedar, would probably have been bought pre-primed. They were easily stored in travelling boxes while wet, making them highly transportable—an important criterion given the conditions under which they were executed. A photograph of Tardieu in military uniform painting *en plein air* (in the open air) at the hospital in the oatfield shows him standing, balancing a portable paint box in one hand and brush in the other, touching up a panel as he scrutinises the scene in the distance. Another shows Tardieu standing in front of a low barn, with a portable easel propping up a painted canvas. Each of the ten paintings in this collection is signed, dated, and marked with its location, so we can consider them 'finished'—even the one that is evidently incomplete (*Unfinished Work—The Artist Astride a Stool*; see Tardieu Oil 4 in the colour section). Tardieu seldom signed his preparatory sketches, especially his more spontaneous and bold experimental works. Certainly his submissions to the *Société des Artistes Français* from 1896 to 1920 show paintings which are much more academic and conservative than his works of the field hospital.

Who could believe, as we looked around the quiet country fields being ploughed, birds building nests, larks soaring in the air— that the greatest war in history was being fought out, that Death and Desolation were blotting out Nature's beauty and depriving the world of the best of its manhood?
—Anon, author of *A War Nurse's Diary*

Close examination of these works reveals a wealth of detail. For example, one of the later paintings, dated September 1915, *Boy Asleep in a Tent* (see Tardieu Oil 10), is an exterior view into the rounded end of a canvas tent. The steep-pitched roof is supported by poles planted into the earth, each pole capped by a rounded finial and secured with guy ropes, suggested by thin brush marks. Inside the tent is a raised wooden floor supporting an iron bed where a young patient sleeps under a pile of bed linen. Across the patient's shoulders lies a bright red shawl, falling to the ground; the red is reflected in the patient's heightened colour which Tardieu emphasises by using viridian green for his pillow. The red-striped awnings hung from the roof seem almost decorative as they loop like curtains across a drawing room, keeping the sun off the bed. Tardieu contrasts the direct sunlight that washes out colour with the light falling through the canvas of the tent, which mottles and transforms what lies beneath into shades of blue, lilac and grey. A bedside locker is bleached by the glare of the sun, the front coloured and shaded to indicate its contents. On the locker is a vase of bright flowers and a bottle on a tray; on the stool beside the bed lies a pile of books and magazines. To the far right of the tent is an open area marking out the field, going up to a horizon of trees. Here Tardieu creates an atmospheric effect by using very thin paint for the sky, mere smudges of blue and lilac against the wooden panel which remains exposed in places, creating haloes around the green trees. Tardieu uses this technique in several of the paintings, leaving the warm orange colour of the panel exposed, in order to separate blocks of colour or to emphasise contrasting areas.

We were placed in [the] charge of the Duchess of Sutherland, who had a hospital unit at St Malo, a suburb of Dunkerque. Arrived there we spent the next day and night at the St Malo Hotel. The Germans gave us a warm reception that night; a squadron of airplanes bombarded Dunkerque, shelling the quays where the ammunition was stored. We leaned out of [the] window, gazing over the sea at the battle in the air, listening the while to loud explosions.

—Anon, author of *A War Nurse's Diary*

Tardieu obviously admired the work of the Duchess of Sutherland at the hospital, and this comes across clearly in the only one of these paintings which depicts her, the painting entitled *Millicent, Duchess of Sutherland Attending to her Patients* (see Tardieu Oil 1). His low viewpoint, looking up at the Duchess, makes her strikingly tall, an effect reinforced by the patients lying below. Millicent stands erect, tray in hand, as she gazes across the ward. Tardieu has depicted her in charge, in control, and in command of herself and her domain. A 'halo' effect around her headdress separates her from the canvas ceiling, which is so sparingly painted that the wood grain of the panel beneath can still be seen. The Duchess is resplendent in white uniform, which Tardieu paints with hints of lavenders, pale greens and pinks, with highlights of white, an echo of the play of light falling through the canvas.

Throughout the series, Tardieu's handling of colour is striking. In the painting of the Duchess the tent top is thinly painted in the palest of lavenders, pinks, oranges and greens, indicating the seeping sunlight pouring through the roof, which has been camouflaged by green paint. At the sides are the striped awnings from seafront hotels used to brighten and extend the tent,

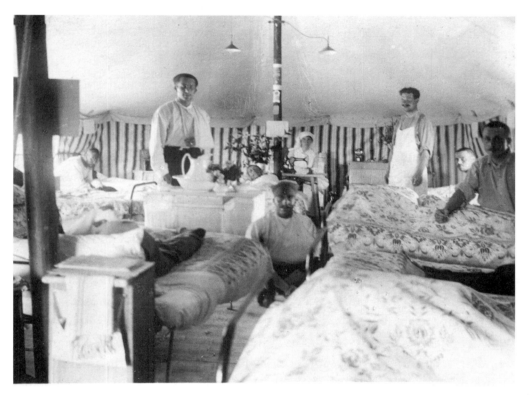

Cramped conditions in the wards, Bourbourg, 1915. This invites direct comparison with Tardieu's paintings. Patients' notes can be seen hanging above the beds. Photographer: Oswald Gayer Morgan. Reproduced by courtesy of Louise and Robert Skioldebrand.

which Tardieu paints as red stripes against pale lilacs, pinks and greens to represent the discoloured white material. The whole effect is a burst of mellow light infiltrating the tent which he contrasts with the sunshine outside, seen through the tent opening on the right. Also visible are the guy ropes secured between flowers and a path leading to another massive tent with a glimpse of a pale lilac-grey sky beyond.

During fine weather, both furniture and patients were moved outside into the sunshine. The patient's pose echoes Tardieu Oil 8. Photographer: Oswald Gayer Morgan. Reproduced by courtesy of Louise and Robert Skioldebrand.

The series of photographs taken by the hospital surgeon Oswald Gayer Morgan gives a striking but different visual record of the camp. The most obvious difference is that these are sepia prints, providing a stark contrast to the vivid colours in Tardieu's paintings. The photographs show the size, scale and diversity of the camp at Bourbourg and the rudimentary nature of its living conditions. They give a sense of vast series of tents with their heavy guy ropes, of tubs of flowers between sparse vegetation, and duckboards thrown along sandy paths and in the midst of the sea of oats growing between the tents. We see the staff having tea, posing for their photograph; nurses hanging out washing next to a Harrods crate which has been sent filled with supplies and perhaps a few luxuries (see page 86); a nurse washing her hair—which begs the question of how the nurses managed to present themselves in pristine white uniforms under these conditions. These details show the quotidian life of the field hospital, whereas Tardieu's paintings, with their bright colours and optimistic disposition, are necessarily selective and romanticised in comparison with Morgan's photographic record.

Morgan's photographs captured the cramped conditions of the wards, with beds abutting against one another. This lack of space is also well-illustrated in several of Tardieu's paintings that show views from inside a tent ward, looking out across a series of beds through the tent flaps to the outside. In *View from Tent of Patients Convalescing in Deckchairs* (see Tardieu Oil 7), Tardieu uses a succession of horizontal and vertical lines of the bed frames and table surface to indicate recession: the frames and edges of the beds and table make a geometric sequence which the eye has to negotiate to reach the distant chateau beyond. This gives the viewer the impression of having to circumnavigate the beds, of moving among the patients as the eye travels through the painting. Tardieu gives a sense of a permeable space where a thin sheet of canvas separates the inside from the outside world. This permeability is also captured in Morgan's photograph showing an occasion when the ward has come outside into the sunshine—a patient sits on a camp bed with his arm in a sling posing for the photographer, echoing the patient's pose in Tardieu's painting *Soldier with Arm in Sling, Seated on a Camp Bed with a Fellow Patient* (see Tardieu Oil 8).

The importance of the gardens, flowers and fresh air is stressed by nursing sister Kate Luard in a letter in April 1916 from a Casualty Clearing Station:

> We had all the acute surgical out in their beds in the sun to-day, in the school yard, round the one precious flower-bed, where are wallflowers and pansies. They enjoy it very much, and smoke, and have their meals out and the gramophone, and it does them a lot of good. They say it shortens the night. 'It does be long sometimes,' said a boy from Cork with a horrid wound in the knee .... We went for a jolly walk after tea in the woods, found violets, cowslips and anemones.

Morgan's photographs highlight the ethnic diversity of the soldiers, men from the colonies who fought alongside the Belgian, French and British military. This diversity is also suggested in Tardieu's paintings such as *Patient with Head Injury and Seated Man with Uniform Cap* (see Tardieu Oil 3). The anonymous author of *A War Nurse's Diary: Sketches from a Belgian Field Hospital*, 1918, who worked in a similar hospital, writes: 'Not only did we nurse the French "poilu", but amongst them were representatives from all the French colonies, black, brown and yellow men .... These poor fellows could not even speak French, and they suffered bitterly from the cold.' Viewing Morgan's photographs in conjunction with Tardieu's paintings invites a richer and more meaningful interpretation of the history of the hospital camp.

Tardieu presented his ten paintings to the Duchess with a touching and intimate dedication painted on the front of her picture: '*à Madame la Duchesse M de Sutherland / Hommage respectueux et tres reconnaissant / d'un simple soldat / Victor Tardieu / Bourbourg Aout 1915*' ('To *Madame La Duchesse*, a respectful

The armies of the main belligerents of the First World War included soldiers from their wider empires. Bourbourg camp 1915. Photographer: Oswald Gayer Morgan. Reproduced by courtesy of Louise and Robert Skioldebrand.

and very grateful tribute from a simple soldier, Victor Tardieu, Bourbourg, August 1915'). The paintings were clearly valued by Millicent, as they were in her apartment in Paris when she died in 1955, and although they remained with the Sutherland family, they were not itemised in the inventory of their estate. The paintings were auctioned in 2011, and acquired by the Abbott and Holder Gallery, where Philip Athill and Tom Edwards researched their history and provenance extensively, creating the excellent and informative Millicent Sutherland Ambulance website. The paintings were purchased by the Florence Nightingale Museum in 2013.

After the war, in 1920, Tardieu was awarded the *Prix de l'Indochine*, allowing him to travel. He never resumed his European career but spent the rest of his life in French Indochina (in an area that is now Vietnam), where he established himself successfully. Official commissions were an important part of his work, including two large-scale murals at the University of Hanoi—in the main lecture hall of the school of medicine and in the reading room of the central library. While continuing to receive official commissions, Tardieu painted the locality around Hanoi, the mountain landscapes, local markets, fishermen and other people, working in palettes of browns and ochres rather than in the brighter colours he had used at the hospital camp. He became involved with local artists and lobbied the colonial government and the government in France to establish a school of fine art based on the École des Beaux-Arts in Paris. In 1925 Tardieu became the first director of the École des Beaux-Arts de l'Indochine in Hanoi, where he remained until his death in 1937.

It is interesting to consider how Tardieu's reputation might have developed if he had remained in France after the war instead of going to Indochina. Perhaps if he had exhibited his more experimental and innovative paintings, he might have become more widely recognised in Europe. However Tardieu's granddaughter indicated that a fire had destroyed much of his work, making it difficult to assess his output and practice or to speculate on his achievement. Unusually, the Bourbourg paintings are signed, dated and marked with their

Tea outside the hospital tents, Bourbourg camp, 1915. Photographer: Oswald Gayer Morgan. Reproduced by courtesy of Louise and Robert Skioldebrand.

location, which suggests these works held a significance for the artist, perhaps reflecting the conditions under which they were produced.

Tardieu's paintings provide a different perspective from the grim sepia world we often associate with images of the First World War. The panels are surprisingly unlike much 'war art' of the time; vibrant, colourful and optimistic, they show men recuperating and recovering in a bright and sunny oatfield in France. There are flowers on bedside lockers, books and magazines, and patients sunning themselves on beds or deckchairs. The tubs and gardens of flowers are all indications that this was not a transit camp but intended to provide a more permanent, stable environment than its brief existence would indicate. Tardieu's paintings do not depict the horrors of war, but a hospital with therapeutic values, a sense of domesticity and well-being. The scene seems remote from the front line, and yet it was so close that the camp's inhabitants would at times have heard the guns and artillery exploding, a reminder of the battlefield to which many of them would be ordered to return.

Perhaps the optimism of these paintings reflects a mood at the beginning of the war, before the fighting descended into the state of motionless attrition which characterised its later course. Tardieu seems to be celebrating the hospital and its staff who are putting their own lives at risk to help the suffering of those at war. These exquisite yet under-recognised paintings give this temporary hospital a degree of permanence, celebrating the determination of those who, like Millicent, Duchess of Sutherland, worked tirelessly to create and sustain voluntary hospitals on battlefield fronts across France. Victor Tardieu remains relatively unknown in this country, and these recently discovered paintings provide an opportunity to draw attention to his work.

7

The Stylish Nurse 1914-1918

·•·

Frederic A Sharf and Jill Carey

The generally accepted image of the First World War nurse is dictated by the handsome wartime posters—she is a saintly vision all in white. In reality, the thousands of nurses who served in France between 1914 and 1918 were attired in outfits that reflected the fashions of the day, as well as being a badge of honour marking them out as contributing to the war effort rather than staying in civilian life. Nurses from many nations, including America, Australia, Canada, France and Britain, served in the war with each nationality having their own regulation uniform, usually consisting of a blue or grey work dress with a white apron and cap. The clothing they wore reflected not only their shared identity as nurses, but also the natural desire of young women to be à la mode.

The various outfits owned by the American nurse Helen Jordan provide us with a fascinating example of the wardrobe of a nurse in the First World War. Helen volunteered at the age of 30 in October 1916 to join the third instalment of the Harvard Surgical Unit, usually referred to simply as the

Massachusetts General Hospital Nursing badge. Reproduced by courtesy of Harvard Medical School Archives Collection.

Harvard Unit. She was a trained nurse, having graduated from the nursing school at Massachusetts General Hospital in Boston. Bostonians in general, and the faculty of Harvard University in particular, became involved in the war (emotionally, physically and financially) well before America formally declared war in April 1917. In 1915 the Harvard professor A Piatt Andrews organised the American Field Service, a volunteer ambulance service staffed by American college students and funded by wealthy Bostonians. In the same year, Boston ladies became involved in the American Fund for French Wounded. This organisation provided medical supplies and bandages to hospitals in France. Society ladies personally made the bandages, usually in sociable groups.

Early in 1915 the eminent British physician Sir William Osler met in London with the Harvard-educated philanthropist Robert Bacon to urge Harvard University to provide a medical team to work in hospitals set up by the British Expeditionary Force in France. The first Harvard Surgical Unit was quickly organised. The university appointed a Unit Manager, Herbert H White, to make all arrangements for supplies, uniforms, recruiting and travel. White ran the unit in a thoroughly business-like manner travelling frequently to London and even to Flanders.

The hospital—a sort of monotone, a place of whispers and wheels moving on rubber tyres, long corridors, and strangely unsexed women moving in them. Unsexed not in any real sense, but the white clothes, the hidden hair, the stern white collar just below the chin, give them an air of school-girlishness, an air and a look women don't wear in the world.

They seem unexpectant. —Enid Bagnold, VAD nurse, author of *A Diary Without Dates*

In June 1915, 32 surgeons, three dentists, and 75 nurses sailed for England. This unit was assigned to General Hospital 22 in the fields of Flanders. Helen voyaged to London in her own daytime clothing. On deck at sea the nurses relaxed in leisure outfits, and she did not acquire the clothing she would need to serve in France until she arrived. Once in London, nurses went to a tailor for a fitting, and a few days later their dress uniforms were delivered to their hotel. Before Helen departed from England for France, she came upon a prominent statue of Florence Nightingale at Waterloo Place on Pall Mall. We can only imagine the feelings of the young nurse, excited yet nervous and far from home, departing from the fitting of her first military nurse uniform and happening on the statue of that most famous of military nurses, a stone's throw from the tailor's shop in Regent's Street. Did Miss Nightingale, looking down stony-faced from her pediment, inspire and give reassurance to Helen? We can only conjecture.

As a member of an independent unit working under the auspices of the American Red Cross, Helen wore regulation US Red Cross uniform. Her dress uniform was a two-piece navy-blue wool twill dress with appliqué details, self-covered buttons and a cotton lining. The shoulder had the Harvard Unit insignia, and she would also have worn her graduate nursing badge. The uniform had a matching cape and hat. The higher waist, cummerbund-enhanced skirt and more relaxed fit of the dress established a silhouette that was similar to everyday attire for women during the war. Her work uniform was a long-sleeved blue cotton dress, and a white starched cotton apron with an embroidered red cross. This outfit would have been worn with a white linen headscarf and a white cotton armband embroidered with 'H U' (for Harvard Unit). There was a third component to her wardrobe: clothing for leisure wear. Helen went to the Regent Street tailor, H J Nicoll & Co, for her dress uniform, and to Harrods on Brompton Road for her work uniform; her leisure outfits may also have been sourced at Harrods. They advertised 'a shirt in fine white linen, perfectly cut and carefully tailored', which would have been ideal for days off. Their advertisements also proclaimed their clothing to be 'Red Cross Regulation'. In a later diary entry of 31st May 1917, Helen's description of the dress of army nurses includes this symbolic detailing: 'They are wearing white uniforms, blue army capes with red linings and small red crosses on the left hand side.'

Helen's diary entry for 4th December, 1916 reads: 'Shopping

Nurse's dress uniform, 1916. This dress uniform belonged to Helen Jordan, who joined the volunteer Harvard Unit in France in 1916. It was purchased from Nicoll & Co on Regent Street. Reproduced by courtesy of Harvard Medical School Archives Collection.

Men hanging fabric in the drying room at the premises of H J Nicoll & Company on Regent Street, London, 2nd January 1913. Reproduced by permission of English Heritage.

all morning .... I bought great heavy tan boots. Am having them oiled ready for service. Also, heavy underclothing .... We had our fittings at Nicoll's and our dark-blue uniforms and cape are very smart. We expect to feel quite proud in them.'

Her shopping expeditions probably also yielded the supplementary cotton work dress with long sleeves in which she was often photographed. Such a dress would have the advantage of being easy to wash. In fact, one of her first activities on her arrival in France was to go to the nearby village and make arrangements with a local woman to do her washing. Footwear for everyday use consisted of short leather lace-up shoes, usually brown. She was thus very practical in her clothing yet her diaries also show a clear interest in being stylish. To be a nurse in 1914-1918 was an occupation which people looked up to, and Helen was always careful to look the part. For all her activities, work and leisure, she needed to dress in professional yet smart clothing.

The most remarkable aspect of Helen's uniform was how closely it mirrored contemporary female style. As with leisure wear, the skirts were shorter than those worn in the previous decade and the fabrics were commonly used materials such as woollen serge and cotton crepe. She brought with her a bathing suit, probably a one-piece wool suit, such as had become popular in the first decade of the twentieth century. All nurses also had a raincoat, modelled on the style of the men's trench coats and usually single breasted.

The normal outfit of a night nurse on winter duty consists of woollen garments piled on cocoon-like under her dress, a jersey over the dress and under the apron or overall, another jersey above the apron, a greatcoat, two pairs of stockings, service boots or gum boots with a pair of woolly soles, a sou'wester, mittens or gloves (perhaps both) and a scarf. —Olive Dent, VAD nurse, author of *a vad in france*

A SUNNY DAY

Keeping a uniform clean and white when nursing in the field was an ongoing challenge. Illustration by R M Savage 'and others', Olive Dent's *A VAD in France*, 1917.

The Harvard Unit was assigned to serve at General Hospital No 22, which was located at Camiers, along the Flanders seacoast close to Boulogne. The Royal Army Medical Corps had taken over many acres of wheatfields on which they constructed a series of tented hospitals. Each hospital was set up to accommodate 1040 beds. As the war lengthened and the casualties increased dramatically, these hospitals expanded. By the time Helen Jordan arrived, the capacity of each hospital was close to 2000 beds. Nursing duties were divided between a day and a night shift, usually with one nurse and an orderly on duty, although sometimes two nurses took the duty instead. Night duty was required of everyone, as convoys with wounded soldiers tended to arrive from 6pm onwards. Helen sometimes had as many as 30 patients to tend to on her own, and her work included making beds, dressing wounds and responding to injuries received from artillery, bombing, poison gas, vehicle accidents and hand-to-hand fighting. On April 3rd 1917 Helen's detailed diary talks of '... doing dressings and trying to make the lads warm and comfortable', and on 20th March 1918 she speaks of there being many gas cases. The main object of the hospital was to move the wounded out as soon as possible, either home to 'Blighty' or back to service. In one ten-day period Helen notes the hospital had received 9000 wounded and moved 8000 out.

It was not all hard work, however. Helen's diary also records the regular activities, which took place outside the hospital ward. Dancing in the hospital mess hall was a common evening occurrence while bicycling through the fields was a popular daytime activity. In the summer, Helen went to the nearby beach for swimming; and she played tennis on courts built within the hospital compound.

Two nurses hanging up laundry at Bourbourg camp, 1915. A nearby crate is labelled 'Harrods' from the famous London shop. Photographer: Oswald Gayer Morgan. Reproduced by courtesy of Louise and Robert Skioldebrand.

Since recreation was an important aspect of life at a military hospital, many American hospitals were equipped with indoor facilities for films, dances, lectures and concerts; as well as outdoor facilities for tennis and other games. The nurses were young and loved the variety of activities in the hospitals. A few quotes from Helen's diary will help the reader to picture the social life. On 16th July, 1917 she writes: 'We bicycled to the beach, taking bathing suits and raincoats; we dressed in the laundry room of the café.' On 2nd August, 1917 she writes: 'We danced in the men's mess. The Canadian orchestra played.' Helen also describes a minstrel show, and a Halloween party: 'Great preparations for a Halloween party tonight. I am going as a Daughter of the Revolution and will wear my little blue silk dress with a kerchief.' It is hard to imagine how Helen managed to have such an elegant dress stored in the limited space allotted to each nurse.

Early in January 1919, General Hospital 22 was busy organising its closure. Helen needed to collect her washing from the village laundress and pack her uniforms into a duffel bag. On Sunday 5th January 1919, she records in her diary that her packing was complete. She also remarks: 'We are leaving the biggest thing of our lives, and we have lived it all.' Later, on 21st January 1919, her thoughtful diary entry notes: 'It may have been misery for some of the boys, but for me it was a privilege to have been part of it … there are regrets at leaving it all behind.' Not only was Helen leaving a work experience that she enjoyed, but she was leaving behind the status that her occupation conveyed. Her attire, whether ceremonial, working, or leisure conveyed this sense of status. She was always a 'stylish nurse.'

8

All the Living and all the Dead
How the First World War Changed our View of Death

•◆•

Holly Carter-Chappell

The First World War is a conflict infamous for its colossal death toll, and the devastating nature of the injuries inflicted on surviving men. As discussed in the previous chapters, nurses were at the forefront of providing medical care and comfort to injured and dying soldiers. The VAD nurses in particular often came from sheltered backgrounds and were drawn to nursing as a way of contributing to the war effort and helping the wounded men in a way they couldn't help their own loved ones serving at the Front. Frequently their only previous nursing experience had been tending to family members during times of sickness. Even the professional nurses found themselves faced with a level of human suffering quite unlike anything they had needed to deal with in their usual working lives; for the VADs the shock of what they encountered must have been enormous. The traditional Victorian ideal of a peaceful 'good death' was unrealistic in the best circumstances; in the chaos and mud of the front line it was non-existent. Nevertheless, as much as possible the nurses working in Casualty Clearing Stations and field hospitals ensured that the men in their care were given respect and dignity and, most importantly, not left alone as they died. Nurses cared for the dying on a daily basis and stood as first-hand witnesses to how the practicalities of war were changing the Victorian social norms surrounding death and memorialisation.

Between 1914 and 1919 there were an estimated 16.5 million military and civilian deaths directly related to the war. In his 2007 autobiography *The Last Fighting Tommy*, First World War veteran Harry Patch describes the war as

'... nothing better than legalised mass murder'. The catastrophic death rate of the First World War coupled with the fact that there was often no body for the families to bury meant that the social norms could no longer be observed to their usual extent. The hasty wartime rituals were very different from what Professor James Stevens Curl terms the Victorian celebration of death.

Death was ever present in Victorian Britain. The infant mortality rate was incredibly high: in 1901 one baby in four died before his or her first birthday; whilst the average life expectancy in 1850 was just 40 years of age. For the poorest in society being able to pay for funerals was a constant worry. A Victorian funeral demonstrated social standing and worth in a class-delineated society. A family unable to pay for a burial would have to suffer the indignity of knowing their loved one had had a pauper's burial in a communal grave. Being able to afford family funerals was of such concern to the working classes that burial clubs were set up by insurance companies; these continued to be popular amongst the working classes into the Edwardian era.

It becomes almost monotonous to tell you again that all those hundreds and hundreds of men we nursed were far spent—suffering from shock collapse, excessive haemorrhage, broken to pieces, many mortally wounded, all in agony, suffering from cold, hunger, exposure to winter weather, frost bite, and every evil that can bring strong men to death's door.
—Anon, author of *A War Nurse's Diary*

Christianity played a central part in the lives of most middle- and upper-class Victorians, and this directly fed into the concept of a 'good death'. A good Christian death required the dying person to be prepared, pious, lucid, and above all ready to embrace salvation. The reality was, of course, often very different from the romanticised ideal and a good death was almost impossible for the poorest and most vulnerable in society to achieve.

Towards the end of the nineteenth century and into the Edwardian age the Victorian way of death began slowly to change. This change was driven by two primary factors: the decline in religious belief and an improvement in mortality rates. From 1870 onwards, church attendance ceased to keep up with population growth, and the popularity of secular works such as Charles Darwin's *On the Origin of Species* (1859) contributed to a more ambivalent approach to religion. At the same time, widespread public health reforms, led by campaigners such as Florence Nightingale, together with improved diet and sanitation, meant life expectancy in England and Wales increased to 52 for men and 55 for women by 1912. The vast majority of those needing care were nursed at home, usually by family members, due both to the prohibitive cost of a doctor and the perceived shame of entering a hospital, which was intrinsically linked with the workhouse in the Victorian and Edwardian psyche. This traditional way of caring for those coming to the end of their lives began to change at the beginning of the twentieth century, as death became increasingly medicalised and moved from the home into hospitals.

The act of nursing the sick and dying had been connected with religion for centuries. Medieval hospitals were religious establishments with care given by monks or nuns, and many of Britain's most well-known hospitals, such as St Bartholomew's and the Bethlem Royal Hospital, both in London, were founded as religious institutions. Often these religious communities would be the only ones willing to take in those suffering from stigmatised diseases such as leprosy or mental health issues. This association with religion continued well into the nineteenth century. The earliest nursing communities in Britain were the Anglican nursing sisterhoods, notably the sisterhood at St John's House in London, which was founded in 1848 and went on to offer nursing services to Charing Cross Hospital. Florence Nightingale spent several months training at the Institute of Deaconesses in Kaiserswerth, Germany, a Lutheran religious community committed to nursing work. It is no coincidence that the first party of 38 nurses Nightingale took to the Crimea in 1854 included fourteen Anglican sisters and ten Roman Catholic nuns. With Nightingale's reforms leading

Both professional and volunteer nurses found themselves caring for men with injuries far removed from their previous experience. Man with bandaged face, Bourbourg camp, 1915. Photographer: Oswald Gayer Morgan. Reproduced by courtesy of Louise and Robert Skioldebrand.

to the professionalisation of nursing in the late nineteenth century, nursing moved into a secular arena while still retaining some of the spiritual emphasis of the early nursing sisterhoods. Nurses increasingly trained and worked independently of religious institutions; however the connection between religion and the act of nursing persisted in popular culture, and even today, many modern nurses see their profession as a vocation or 'calling'. Nurses in the early decades of the twentieth century embodied both a scientific approach to disease while still conforming to the model of the 'angel of mercy', there to selflessly bring help and comfort to those in most need.

The increased religious ambivalence in the late Victorian and Edwardian period had several unintentional consequences, chiefly the rise of cremation as an alternative to burial and a growing interest in spiritualism, which was to be of huge significance to mourning during and after the First World War. Spiritualists believed in the immortality of the soul and the possibility of communication with the dead through mediums. The spiritualist movement began in the United States in the 1840s and gained popularity in Britain during the 1860s. In 1890 an American businessman, Elijah Bond, began selling Ouija boards as a parlour game; it was not until the First World War, however, that the American medium Pearl Curran popularised them as a tool for contacting the spirit

Today [1933], tours of the battlefields in France are arranged by numerous agencies; graves are visited in parties, and a regular trade has been established in wreaths and photographs and cemeteries. But that level of civilisation had not been reached in 1921, so Winifred [Holtby] and I hired a car in Amiens, and plunged through a series of shell-racked roads between the grotesque trunks of skeleton trees, with their stripped, shattered branches still pointing to heaven in grim protest against man's ruthless cruelty to nature as well as man. —**Vera Brittain, VAD nurse, author of** *Testament of Youth*

world. The decline in conventional religious belief was greatly accelerated by the outbreak of the First World War, thirteen years after the death of Queen Victoria, in August 1914. Church attendance dropped steeply, as families struggled to reconcile the loss of their sons and brothers with the idea of an all-powerful, benevolent God. As organised religion faltered, the spiritualist movement gained a huge following from bereaved relatives desperate for some sign that their husbands and brothers lived on.

The elaborate death rituals of the pre-war period were adapted by necessity during the war. Mourning dress was simplified; the heavy crape dress and veil, made so iconic by Queen Victoria, had already begun to fall out of fashion by the turn of the twentieth century. In addition to this, the First World War saw a reduction in the amount of time society expected a woman to wear mourning. This was due in part to the fear that thousands of young women wearing widow's weeds would have a negative effect on the nation's morale, and also partly to the practicalities of many women having taken on war work. Nursing uniform was worn with pride and seen as a symbol of the wearer's patriotism and honour. A black armband might be worn when a nurse had suffered the death of a

In a conflict where many families had no grave to visit, civic memorials were of huge importance. This photograph shows memorial wreaths at the Cenotaph in 1921, the year after it was unveiled. Reproduced by permission of English Heritage.

loved one, but with a shortage of trained nurses and an overwhelming number of casualties, a nurse had little time to mourn. Many nurses simply carried on with their work after a bereavement, perhaps finding an inner strength in the knowledge that their work was helping to ensure other women did not suffer the same loss.

The First World War, a time of great patriotism and militaristic pride, saw a significant reduction in elaborate funeral ceremonies and mourning rituals observed by the general population, partly because the War Office banned the repatriation of the dead in 1915. Many civilians were therefore reluctant to continue to mark the passing of their loved ones in the grandiose ways of the pre-war period, when all too often the families of fighting men did not have the comfort of a body to bury at all. Nurses were often a family's only source of information about their relation's death; they were routinely the person by a dying soldier's side in Casualty Clearing Stations or field hospitals. The War Office would send a telegram informing the soldier's family of his death, but it was the nurses who could provide the comforting details all families wanted to know: who held his hand at the last or whether he experienced much pain. An anonymous nurse who later published an account of her experiences in a Belgium field hospital movingly writes of a widow visiting the hospital where her husband had died: 'How could I have told her of her loved one's sufferings? She wanted his last words, but he did not even realise he was dying. There was little it was possible to tell her, while as to his grave, in those early days it was difficult to find individual graves. Graves were

Nursing on the front line was a dangerous occupation. During the First World War hundreds of military nurses attached to the British Army made the ultimate sacrifice. This photograph shows the funeral of an army nurse killed during an air raid on a British Military Hospital in France. © Imperial War Museums Q11034.

there in plenty, by the hundreds and thousands, but which one ...' Christine Hallett in *Containing Trauma* (2009) tells of Sister Kate Luard who wrote to the bereaved wife of one of her patients and received the response 'If it is possible to gain any comfort in my agonising loss, you have given it me. I sent flowers addressed to you for his grave because I felt that you would of your goodness lay them on my hero's grave.'

The impact and trauma Britain suffered as the result of the catastrophic death toll was unprecedented, and for us, looking back a hundred years later, hard to comprehend. The mechanised nature of modern warfare meant that tens of thousands of men could be killed during a single battle. During the Battle of the Somme, for example, it is estimated that over 300,000 Allied and German service personnel lost their lives, with 19,240 British and Commonwealth servicemen dying on the first day alone. There was rarely time to retrieve the bodies of the fallen, and their comrades would have to leave them where they fell.

Belgium, September 1914.
We passed lots of Germans, but none spoke to us, and now we went over the battlefield. There were graves at the side with roughly made crosses. A house ruined by a shell, the front gone, all ruin, again saw trenches with odd knapsacks, a soldier playing the piano outside a ruined cottage...
—Muriel Bartlett, one of the Sutherland Ambulance Unit's nurses. Unpublished diary

Almost every young woman would have lost a brother, father, uncle or friend during the course of the four-year conflict, providing many young women with their inspiration to nurse. Mourning was a communal, almost universal experience and there was the sense that all these brave brothers in arms were now equal in death, whatever their social standing may have been in life. As J M Winter put it in his 1987 work *The Great War and the British People*, 'The individuality of death had been buried under literally millions of corpses.'

From the opening months of the war, communities had looked for ways to remember their dead, with makeshift shrines being created, often in association with a church, and then becoming a focus for religious services and donations towards the war effort. Early official war memorials in Britain had been closely linked with military recruitment; perversely, if a local recruitment office had met its targets then a community could be awarded a memorial to their dead. By the declaration of the Armistice in November 1918, the collective mourning of the nation created a need to commemorate and eulogise the sacrifice of so many courageous men. The most common source of funding for memorials was public subscription, and their construction would often be organised by a committee designed to represent all sections of the local community. These memorials took on a particular significance for the families of those men whose bodies had never been found or identified, as it gave them a focus for their grief. By the end of the First World War, several hundred military nursing personnel had also lost their lives during the course of their work through shelling, drowning, infection, accident and disease. There is no specific memorial to the British nurses who died during the war, although individual nurses are honoured on local war memorials, and many who died overseas are buried in one of the military cemeteries, their final resting place marked by a white Commonwealth War Graves Commission headstone. Following the war the British government issued memorial plaques to the next of kin of all British and Empire service personnel killed as a consequence of the war. The plaques were designed by Edward Carter Preston, cast in bronze and had a diameter of 5 inches; their resemblance to the penny coin earning them the popular nickname of 'Deadman's Penny'. These medallions were manufactured into the 1930s, as men continued to die due to injuries sustained during the conflict. It is estimated that a total of 1,355,000 plaques were issued, over 600 of them for women.

In 1918 the challenges the war presented to nursing staff were compounded by the outbreak of an influenza pandemic. Its rapid spread was due in part to troop movements; many nurses found themselves particularly at risk of contracting the disease as they cared for their patients, and a number of nurses died. Red Cross VAD Margaret van Straubenzee wrote of how when she contracted influenza she carried on with her duties for as long as possible before collapsing with a temperature of 103 degrees. Although the total number of deaths from the 1918-19 influenza pandemic is estimated to be at least twice that of the First World War, it has been, as historian Alice Reid puts it, 'rapidly relegated to obscurity'. The pandemic struck in three distinct waves with the first and third being comparatively mild while the second proved cataclysmic, spreading with terrifying speed and killing large numbers of the young and previously healthy. Even today, in the twenty-first century, antiviral medication is still very much in its infancy. A hundred years ago, there was very little treatment available, other than fluids and bed rest. Britain's hospitals were filled with war casualties and at least half the nation's doctors and professional nurses were in military service, leaving limited resources to nurse the civilian population. The speed with which the illness struck and killed was staggering: there are anecdotes of victims complaining of a headache at dinner and being dead by morning. The huge death toll, combined with the already short supply of able-bodied men, was

Drug manufacturers were quick to find a way of turning public concern about the influenza pandemic into profit. As seen in this example of an advertisement for 'Formamint', a lozenge believed to stop the spread of the disease. Published in The Sphere magazine, 1918. Private Collection / © The Advertising Archives / The Bridgeman Art Library.

overwhelming for undertakers and gravediggers and resulted in bodies often remaining in homes for a considerable period of time, in some cases up to a fortnight, further exposing family members to the risk of infection.

The First World War was a conflict which changed the very nature of warfare and the way in which we respond to it. The scale of the death and destruction left in its wake is seared on British collective memory; and on Remembrance Day each year the country stops to commemorate the fallen. However, the second decade of the twentieth century was also a time of great social change, especially for women. Many previously sheltered young women rose magnificently to the challenge of nursing the wounded and often traumatised young men who came into their care. The VAD ranks were filled with women who had not only had no experience of nursing, but also no practical experience of work at all; suddenly they were expected to comfort dying men, clean gangrenous wounds and often improvise with very little equipment and few supplies. During and after the First World War, the previously observed rituals surrounding death and mourning, which had been so important, fell by the wayside.

There were no good deaths in the war. Young men were cut down in their tens of thousands, suffering violent and appalling ends, or dying horribly from their wounds in hospital, often with a dedicated nurse the only witness to their agony. However all too frequently no body was recovered and families were left without a grave to visit or sense of closure. After the war the battlefields became places of pilgrimage for the bereaved wishing to be close

Nurses often recorded their experiences during the war in diaries and autograph albums. Today, they provide us with a fascinating insight into their lives. Pencil sketch of wounded soldier and nurse by Mabel Earp, a VAD nurse. Circa 1914-18. Reproduced by courtesy of Cheshire Military Museum.

to their husbands, sons and brothers. Previously, mourning had been about an individual and their social rank. With the entire country in collective mourning for a 'lost generation' of 'brothers in arms', this seemed out of step with the mood of the nation and gradually Britain's mourning culture transformed into the simpler and often secular rituals we recognise today. The way in which the British as a nation view death and commemoration changed forever.

Epilogue

•◆•

The nurses on the battlefields of war-torn France were ordinary women who found themselves in extraordinary circumstances, and they rose to the challenges they met in ways we can only imagine today. From all backgrounds, young and middle-aged, inexperienced debutantes and professional nurses, together they answered the call and experienced every aspect of war in their mission to alleviate suffering. Using every method of innovation open to them, these nurses created the best medical environment they could, whether in a muddy oatfield or on a moving barge, to care for the desperately injured men. Frequently, the extreme pressures and the necessity for experiment in these temporary hospitals meant that major medical advances were made, especially in infection control and the treatment of shock. Lack of medical staff meant that women were needed to fulfil previously male duties such as surgery and anaesthesia, and volunteer nurses were to play a crucial role, supplying trained and dedicated nursing under the guidance of more experienced nurses. Their wartime experiences, although traumatic, painful and often dangerous, shaped their lives and expanded their worlds, and for many, the war was the big adventure of their lives.

'But camp-life in fine weather is glorious—glorious are the nights when the nightingale sings in the forest which borders our camp. Glorious are the times when we lie abed looking out on a moon-bathed sky with scurrying mysterious clouds, nights when we tell ourselves that there is no war. Glorious it is to sit and watch a rose sunset fade to mauve twilight, with a honey-coloured moon, long drawn out nights when one's life has time to pause, and one takes a moment to think. Then one loses the charm, turns sideways in the deck-chair swallowing the lump in one's throat, a lump partly occasioned by the beauty of the evening, partly by one's sheer physical tiredness, and partly by the memory of a torn and gaping wound and of a magnificent young life dying behind a red screen in the ward yonder, quickly as the sunset.'

Olive Dent, VAD

Acknowledgements

The editors would like to thank the following people for their help in the production of this book:

Philip Athill, Julia Brettell, Jill Carey, Jean Carr-Gomm, Holly Carter-Chappell, Simon Chaplin, Theresa Doherty, Katie Edwards, Tom Edwards, Florence Evans, Jonathan Evans, Imogen Gray, Eric Gruber von Arni, Dominick Jones, Danuta Kneebone, Sue Light, Emily Mayhew, Catherine McGregor, Emily Oldfield, Scott Morrison, Jenny Pedre, Frederic A Sharf, Sue Sheridan, Louise Skioldebrand, Robert Skioldebrand, Elizabeth Millicent, Countess of Sutherland, Helen Turner, and the Trustees, staff and volunteers of the Florence Nightingale Museum.

Quotations from Vera Brittain's *Testament of Youth* are included by permission of Mark Bostridge and T J Brittain-Catlin, Literary Executors for the Estate of Vera Brittain 1970.

The editors have made every effort to track down and identify copyright for text and images and would be glad to hear of any examples where they have been unable to attribute copyright correctly.

Bibliography

—◆—

Books

Anonymous, *A War Nurse's Diary: Sketches from a Belgian Field Hospital* (Manchester, The Macmillan Company, 1918)

Bagnold, Enid, *A Diary without Dates* (London, Virago, 1978)

Bennett, Arnold *The Card* (New York, E P Dutton, 1911)

Brittain, Vera *Testament of Youth* (London, Virago, 2004)

Dent, Olive, *A VAD in France* (Grant Richards, 1917)

Gillies, Harold, *Plastic Surgery of the Face* (Oxford, Frowde, 1920)

Hallett, Christine, *Containing Trauma: Nursing work in the First World War* (Manchester University Press, 2009)

Hallett, Christine E, *Veiled Warriors: Allied Nurses of the First World War* (Oxford University Press, 2014)

Jalland, P, *Death in the Victorian Family* (Oxford University Press, 1999)

Jalland, P, *Death in War and Peace: A History of Grief and Loss in England, 1914-1970* (Oxford University Press, 2011)

Jupp, P and Gittings, C, *Death in England: An Illustrated History* (Manchester University Press, 1999)

King, A, *Memorials of the Great War in Britain: The Symbolism and Politics of Remembrance* (Berg Publishers, 1998)

Lamb, Helen Jordan, *An American Nurse with The British Troops in France NOV 1916 - Feb 1919* (Provo, Stevenson's Genealogical Center, 1981)

Lewis-Stempel, J, *Six Weeks: The Short and Gallant Life of the British Officer in the First World War* (London, Orion Books, 2010)

Mayhew, Emily, *Wounded: From Battlefield to Blighty 1914-1918* (London, Bodley Head, 2013)

Patch, Harry and Van Emden, Richard, *The Last Fighting Tommy* (London, Bloomsbury, 2007)

Piggott, Juliet, *Queen Alexandra's Royal Army Nursing Corps* (Barnsley, Leo Cooper, 1975)

Powell, Anne *Women in the War Zone: Hospital Service in the First World War* (Stroud, The History Press, 2009)

Poynter, Denise J, 'The Report on her Transfer was Shell-Shock', unpublished PhD thesis, The University of Northampton, 2008

Roberts, C and Cox, M *Health and Disease in Britain from Prehistory to Present Day* (Stroud, Sutton Publishing, 2003)

Rogers, Anna, *While You're Away: New Zealand Nurses at War 1899-1948* (Auckland University Press, 2003)

Sackville-West, Vita, *The Edwardians* (London, The Hogarth Press, 1930)

Seymer, L R, *A General History of Nursing* (London, Faber & Faber, 1954)

Sharf, Frederic A with Pate, Catherine and Carey, Jill, *The Fashionable Nurse* (2013)

Stuart, Denis, *Dear Duchess: Millicent, Duchess of Sutherland, 1867-1955* (London, Victor Gollancz, 1982)

Sutherland, Millicent, Duchess of, *Six Weeks at the War* (London, The Times, 1914)

Smith, Angela K, '"Beacons of Britishness": British Nurses and Female Doctors as Prisoners of War', in Fell, A S and Hallett, C E (eds) *First World War Nursing: New Perspectives* (London, Routledge, 2013)

Souttar, H S, *A Surgeon in Belgium* (London, Edward Arnold, 1915)

Stobart, Mabel St Clair, *The Flaming Sword in Serbia and Elsewhere* (London, Hodder and Stoughton, 1916)

Thurstan, Violetta, *A Text Book of War Nursing* (London, New York, G P Putnam's Sons, 1917)

Winter, J M, *The Great War and the British People* (London, Macmillan, 1987)

Archives

Bartlett, Muriel, unpublished war diary

Blair, MAC, Reminiscences of a Nursing Sister (1914-1918), Queen Alexandra's Royal Army Nursing Corps (QARANC) Collection

Blundell, Evelyn, Diary—England to Italy, 1918, QARANC Collection

Brown, Dame Sydney, Report on a Visit to France in 1915, QARANC Collection

Chater, Mickey, personal archive, Imperial War Museum

Cliffe, I E, SRN at War: A Nurse's Memoirs of 1914-1918: QARANC Collection

Discussion of the War Office Committee on the Reorganisation of the Army Medical and Nursing Services

Farmborough, Florence, Oral History Interview, 1975; The Liddle Collection, Brotherton Library, University of Leeds

Fitzgerald, Alice, Unpublished Memoirs incorporating War Diary, c 1936; Maryland Historical Society, Baltimore, Maryland, USA

Holden, E, Autograph Album, 3rd (London) General Hospital, Wandsworth, 1914-1918, QARANC Collection

Humphrys, I, Diary, August 1914-September 1915, QARANC Collection

Johnson, Louie, Oral History Interview, 1974, Imperial War Museum

Martin, M, Diary of Sister Mary Martin, 1916-1918, QARANC Collection

McCarthy, Dame Maud, Annual Nursing Reports to CinC for 1914-1919, QARANC Collection

McCarthy, Dame Maud, Reports on Nursing Services: 1918, Army Medical Services Museum

The Morgan photograph albums held by Robert and Louise Skioldebrand

Nelson, Alice Essington, MS account of her work at Princess Louise's Convalescent Home, Imperial War Museum, London

Philips, M, 'Life on an Ambulance Train', Nurses' Accounts, Army Medical Services Museum

Read, R, Diary of Rebecca Jane Read, QAIMNS(R), No 10 Ambulance Train, QARANC Collection

Regulations for the Army Medical Services, 1897 (London, War Office, 1897)

Shingleton, F, Autograph Album, QARANC Collection

Todd, J, The Diary of Sister Jean Todd, RRC, QARANC Collection

Tyers, M, Diary of Miss Mary Tyers, TANS, QARANC Collection

Periodicals

Anonymous, 'Sinking of the *Marquette*' *Marlborough Express*, 24th November 1915

McConnell, M, 'Living on the Front Line: extracts from the diaries of Agnes Cline, 1917', *Nursing Times*, 2nd August 1989

Morgan, Oswald G, 'The Wounded in Namur' in the *British Journal of Surgery*, 1914

Naqvi, NH (1985) 'Bravery and Devotion to Duty, (Ethel Garrett)', *Nursing Times*

Walter, T 'Historical and Cultural Variants on the Good Death' the *British Medical Journal* 327, 2003

Biographies

•◆•

JILL CAREY is an Associate Professor and Curator of the Lasell Fashion Collection at Lasell College. Most recently Carey was promoted to the title of the Joan Weiler Arnow Professor '49, a three-year endowed position awarded for excellence in teaching and community impact. Carey's teaching and research initiatives centre on the relationship between dress and cultural understanding which has provided opportunities for presentations at academic institutions, corporations, and professional conferences. Carey's dual roles as both a mentor and curator have enabled Lasell students to collaborate with professional partners to showcase various topics related to dress. She recently co-authored a book titled *The Fashionable Nurse* (2013).

HOLLY CARTER-CHAPPELL is the Collections Assistant at the Florence Nightingale Museum and co-curator of *The Hospital in the Oatfield: The Art of Nursing in the First World War* exhibition at the museum. She studied Bioarchaeology at the University of Bradford and Death Studies at the Centre for Death and Society, University of Bath. Her research interests include the public perception of the excavation and display of human remains, the legal and ethical issues surrounding the repatriation and reburial of human remains from colonial contexts, and the medicalisation of death during the twentieth century.

SIMON CHAPLIN is a curator turned library director. His background is in the history of science and medicine. As Senior Curator at the Royal College of Surgeons of England he led the redisplay of the Hunterian Museum, leading to its shortlisting for the Gulbenkian Prize in 2006. Since joining the Wellcome Library he has led a major programme of digitisation and the physical development of the library. His research interests include the history of anatomy and cultures of medical collecting and display from the eighteenth century to the present.

ERIC GRUBER VON ARNI served for 31 years as a nursing officer in the medical services of the British army. His final military appointment was as Director of Nursing Studies at the Royal Army Medical College in London. His written works include *Justice to the Maimed Soldier* (Ashgate, 2001), *Hospital Care and the British Standing Army, 1660-1714* (Ashgate, 2006) and he is currently researching a second sequel for this series planned to take his work forward to the late eighteenth century. Dr Gruber von Arni is a Fellow of the Royal Historical Society, and a Research Associate at the Centre for the History of Medicine, University of Oxford.

CHRISTINE HALLETT is Professor of Nursing History at the University of Manchester, and Chair of the UK Association for the History of Nursing. She was founding Chair of the European Association for the History of Nursing and holds Fellowships of both the Royal Society of Medicine and the Royal Society for the Arts. Professor Hallett trained as a nurse and health visitor in the 1980s and practised as a community nurse before becoming a lecturer at the University of Manchester in 1993. Her most recent research has focused on the work of nurses during the First World War, and she has authored several books on the subject. She is historical advisor and script advisor for the BBC First World War drama 'The Crimson Field'.

DANUTA KNEEBONE was born in East Africa, where she spent her childhood. After training as a marine geologist at Manchester University and working for the British Geological Survey, she undertook postgraduate research in South Africa. Changing direction, she then studied with the Open University, gaining a first class degree in Art History and Philosophy. She is currently undertaking an MA in Art History at Birkbeck University, where she studies the intersection between medicine and art and has a specialist interest in the body. Her MA dissertation is on Victor Tardieu's paintings of the Oatfield camp at Bourbourg in 1915.

SUE LIGHT is a trained nurse and midwife who worked as a nursing sister in Queen Alexandra's Royal Army Nursing Corps both in England and abroad. Originally involved with an in-depth study of local war memorials in her home area, an interest in both the history of nursing and the First World War led on to some specialised research into the military nursing services of the early twentieth century, focusing mainly on the Western Front during wartime. Her website Scarlet Finders contains transcriptions and reproductions of many original documents and images.

EMILY MAYHEW is a military medical historian and research associate at Imperial College London. She has written two books: *The Reconstruction of Warriors* (Greenhill 2004) about Archibald McIndoe and the RAF's Guinea Pig Club, and *Wounded: The Long Journey Home from the Great War* (Vintage 2014) which focuses on the casualties of the Western Front and the men and women of the military medical system, including nurses, who fought to save their lives.

NATASHA McENROE is the Director of the Florence Nightingale Museum, and co-curated the exhibition *The Hospital in the Oatfield*. Her previous post was Museum Manager of the Grant Museum of Zoology and Comparative Anatomy and Curator of the Galton Collection at University College London. From 1997–2007, she was Curator of Dr Johnson's House in London's Fleet Street. She co-edited *The Tyranny of Treatment: Samuel Johnson, His Friends and Georgian Medicine* (British Art Journal, 2003).

FREDERIC A SHARF is a well-known collector, scholar and author. He specialises in buying archives of design drawings which he researches and organises for public exhibitions. He has a special connection to the Museum of Fine Arts in Boston. Fred and Jean, his wife of 50 years, have recently established a Design Department at the Museum of Fine Arts, Boston with a funded Curator of Design. This will assure care of the design drawing collection, as well as provide for growth of this collection.